Praise for Connie Steele and *Building the Business of You*

"Connie has outlined an adaptable framework to get you energized and create your perfect career in this practical and engaging book!"
—Chris Krimitsos
Founder, PodfestExpo.com and Author, *Start Ugly*

"I LOVE this book. The information is relevant, thought-provoking, and actionable. Anyone who is considering entrepreneurship should start here!"
—Dr. Richard Shuster
Internationally Renowned Influencer, Host of the Daily Helping Podcast, Media Expert, and TEDx Speaker

"For anyone with an entrepreneurial spirit, this book is the spark you need to ignite your new journey!"
—Cara Siletto
President, Magnet Culture and Author, *Staying Power: Why Your Employees Leave and How to Keep Them Longer*

"Whether you're just starting or wondering if it's too late to start again, Connie will give you perspective, provide inspiration, and help you discover how to find fluidity in your professional world."
—Beth Freedman
CEO, dentsu X

"*Building the Business of You* is a powerful guide to embracing a new way of living out our personal and professional pursuits."
—Catharine Bowman
Vice President, Alberta Lymphedema Association

Building the
Business of
YOU

We have entered the new world of work. Where are you in it—and where do you want to go? Just as importantly, who do you want to be?

Building the
Business of
YOU

A SYSTEM TO ALIGN PASSION AND GROWTH POTENTIAL THROUGH YOUR OWN CAREER MASHUP

Connie Steele

Flywheel Associates, LLC
Lansdowne, VA

Building the Business of You copyright © 2021 by Connie Steele

Flywheel Associates, LLC
18938 Rocky Creek Drive
Leesburg, VA 20176
www.FlywheelAssociates.com
Send feedback to Info@FlywheelAssociates.com

Publisher's Cataloging-In-Publication Data

Names: Steele, Connie, author.
Title: Building the business of you : a system to align passion and
    growth potential through your own career mash-up / Connie Steele.
Description: Lansdowne, Virginia : Flywheel Associates, LLC, [2021] |
    Includes bibliographical references.
Identifiers: ISBN 9781736218402 (softcover paperback) | ISBN 9781736218419
    (case bound hardback) | ISBN 9781736218426 (ebook)
Subjects: LCSH: Vocational guidance. | Occupations. | Flexible work
    arrangements. | Self-employed. | Self-actualization (Psychology)
Classification: LCC HF5381 .S74 2021 (print) | LCC HF5381 (ebook) | DDC
    650.14--dc23

To my future career mashuppers, Dylan and Cameron. I'm in awe of your innate talents and look forward to watching you create worlds of opportunity that leverage all of your interests, passions, and potential.

Let's build the business of you together.

Change is here. Uncertainty is the new certainty. But what happens now . . . and next? Let's continue your journey to get you to where you want to go.

The *Building the Business of You* companion course features instruction from me along with business, communication, and networking experts who offer actionable advice and diverse perspectives from real-world experiences.

In this guided course, we'll dive deeper into the system so you can put these concepts into practice. We'll work through the "how" so you can find your flow and form your unique career mashup. Specifically, you will . . .

- spot the trends so you can identify not just "what" but the "so what" and "now what"
- create your compass (or compasses) to point you where you want to go
- prepare for change so you can push past fear and inertia
- network in a way that builds authentic relationships to support you in your journey
- build the skills to move you towards your goals

Go to www.BizOfYou.co to pick up where this book leaves off and continue aligning your passion, purpose, and potential.

Contents

Preface

Fluidity, the Career Mashup, and Why I Wrote This Book

I knew nothing when I started my career. And I mean nothing. I assumed that if I worked hard, a company would acknowledge my accomplishments. Because businesses are a meritocracy like school, right? Get good grades, get recognition, get to the next level. I assumed my career path would look something like this:

↓ Work hard
↓ Deliver results
↓ Get recognized and rewarded
↓ Move upward and earn compensation
✓ Attain work fulfillment

I was naive and wrong. I knew nothing about the workplace dynamics that determine advancement—or how few of them involved actual *work*.

Growing up in a Chinese immigrant family, my priorities were set toward academic progression and achievement. Everything was pass or fail, right or wrong, black or white. The plan was always a linear one—bachelor's degree, then a master's degree (at a minimum), and then enter the "real world"—because the conventional thinking was that the higher the level of education, the greater the opportunities.

Even in college, the expectation was that I had to decide my major by the end of my freshman year, even though I had no idea what I wanted to do. (How many of us really do?) Up until that point, I had done assistant teaching, math homework grading, retail, and food service.

True to the Asian stereotype, I ended up pursuing a math major and then doing a double major in statistics. Why? My father holds a PhD in statistics, so I was nudged along that route (even though I did try several other quantitative-oriented subjects—and hated them). That was my first experience of testing and learning to at least figure out what I liked and didn't, what I was good at and wasn't.

One afternoon during my junior year, I buried myself in the vocational handbooks at the university library, trying to figure out what I would do with these degrees and what I would even study in a graduate program. (This was a couple of years before Google. Ancient history, I know.) I had to have some idea of what my career path was going to be. There, I discovered a practical statistics application—marketing! I read about how consumer data (such as attitudes, motivations, and behaviors) was used to drive decisions when it came to conceiving, developing, and promoting the common everyday products we see on store shelves. I learned about brand building and what went into building the great brands that we all knew and loved. The specific field that involved collecting and analyzing the data to gather those great insights was marketing research—I had found something that seemed to fit.

I enrolled in a marketing course and loved it. For graduate school, I studied applied statistics (notice the emphasis on "applied") with the goal of being a marketing researcher and specifically working in the consumer packaged goods industry. In the mid- to late 1990s, the top jobs in this field were working for these types of companies, as they were leaders in building strong brands.

So I made it my mission to get an internship with one of these organizations in order to set me down the right course. And I landed one with the top company in the industry. I was ready to show them what I could do. I had the pedigree and work ethic to deliver the goods, right?

Wrong.

The place felt stodgy. Programmatic. I didn't fit. At least I could put my head down and do what I did best—complete my project. I kept my academic mindset, assuming that what my employer wanted was a job well done. That's what I gave them, assuming I would receive a job offer when my internship ended.

No offer came. The research, analysis, and final presentation were seen as excellent work. But my work product wasn't the reason I wasn't offered a job—I never spoke up in meetings or took on (or even proposed) initiatives outside of my main project. I went in thinking the way to achieve was to do as you're told, and that wasn't what they were looking for in an upcoming leader. You had to contribute value differently than what I originally understood.

I hated it there anyway, I told myself. *It wasn't the right fit culturally.*

The experience I gained from this top-tier company did open up a lot of opportunities for full-time jobs, and I successfully landed one from another market leader.

But there I struggled too. Early on, I excelled because it was more structured and defined in terms of what we had to do and how to succeed. When everyone entered the company, the focus was on foundational training—the specific technical skills—all of which was intended to prepare you when you went to the business side of the house. But when I was promoted and transitioned to the next role in the organization, things weren't so black and white for me on how to best perform my role and understand the importance and dynamics of various relationships in the organization.

In fact, I felt unprepared and uncomfortable. I had to learn how to lead and influence in a different way. I couldn't be the doer anymore, and there weren't obvious answers on what methodologies to employ for the various challenges (and opportunities) we had in the business. There were people dynamics that I knew were affecting what we would and should do that put me in uncomfortable situations. These factions and needs among the cross-functional teams had an impact on what the outcome of the data would be. Those feelings from my internship started creeping back in.

But school never taught me how to see the big picture, to learn which players in the game mattered, to understand how to drive others to a common outcome versus being the one being driven, and to handle those ugly politics. I wasn't performing, and my new boss (not a mentor at all) forced my hand to go back to the department where I started or potentially risk being let go. That was seen to some degree as a demotion.

Two essential soft skills that did come naturally to me were asking the right people for advice and building a "village" of said right people. At that point, my coworkers rallied around me. They offered the emotional and professional support that helped me connect the dots in ways that I never understood before.

Mind you, connecting the dots strategically and tactically across the business and the people in it was completely foreign to me. While I'd spent all my time studying consumer attitudes, motivations, and behavior for my profession, I was raised to see the world as binary. The reality is business is shades of gray. In school, I got an A, a B, or a C based on the overall correctness of my answers or adherence to the grading rubric. It's not the same in business. The academic incentives I was used to working for do not exist in the workplace. So I had to shift my focus from acing a test to thinking creatively, adding value, and making an impact, which is defined by each unique situation (company, role, deliverables, relationships, etc.).

The village and new skills I'd formed at the consumer foods company helped elevate me to the next level, but I got bored. The internet was the hot new thing. Food flavors and product packaging were not. I also wanted to bring my right brain to work for once after being forced down the left-brain path for so long. So I left to join one of the internet powerhouses at the time, America Online, AOL for short. It felt like home from the start. There was an openness, creativity, freedom, and flexibility that I had never experienced. Compared to the traditional large corporate structures that I had worked for up until this point, in which there were specific processes and defined groups and hierarchy to everything, this new work environment was one where there weren't clear lines.

We had to understand "the matrix." There wasn't a strict (or even clear) delineation of functions, and you had to work collaboratively with multiple cross-functional and cross-business groups to get the job done. To some degree, we reported to multiple people who were not technically our bosses. Relationships were everything.

Like most technology companies, everything moved fast, so you had to quickly learn to connect the dots and create progress in a way that was a multiple of what I had to deal with earlier.

And there weren't the deeply embedded processes, decision gates, or even data to help drive decisions that I was accustomed to. In fact, much of what we had to do was create along the way. We had the freedom to truly build and implement our ideas. There really wasn't any right or wrong. It was all about developing a plan that made the most business sense based on what the immediate goal was at the time, essentially putting a stake in the ground and developing it *quickly*—speed to market was critical.

I realized later on in my career that AOL was the place where I really developed this test-and-learn approach and mindset. It updated my view of failure. In school, failure was bad. At the large companies I had worked for, you also couldn't fail. But at AOL, we did a lot, and a lot of things didn't always work. But we learned and moved on. It seemed OK to not know everything, because we didn't. In such a progressive and forward-thinking environment, failure is good. Because only through failure did we understand how to improve, iterate, and pivot.

And pivot we did, particularly on an individual level. Layoffs were commonplace, so when we got reorganized, we had to learn a new role, new team, and new part of the business *fast*. We had to build up those hard and soft skills so we could deliver value quickly. And those relationships that had been built over time mattered even more with the constantly changing work environment.

Looking back, I'm fortunate to have worked at large corporations for the first part of my career at a time when structured training and professional development programs were readily available. They taught me valuable skills that I needed. At these companies and subsequent ones, I've had wonderful mentors and colleagues who have become advisors as well as friends. This training, advice, and feedback has guided my journey from being an employee of a company to running my own consulting business. It also helped me understand the all-important soft and hard skills necessary to build momentum that carries you forward in work and in life.

This is where my story and yours intersect—the reason you hold this book in your hands at this moment. In today's rapidly changing work environment, there isn't the same level of investment in employee development (or even any investment at all) despite the need and demand. The formal and informal support structure of years-long mentorships doesn't exist the way it once did. Because of COVID-19, many now work remotely. As a result, many are no longer able to meet face-to-face. The challenge is building authentic relationships virtually, which is difficult for many.

And the average stint at one job drops from one generation to the next. On average, baby boomers stay at one job for eight years, Generation X for 5.4 years, millennials for 2.4 years, and Gen Z for only 1.2 years.[1] Professionals in the first ten years of their career now have to "Frankenstein" the advice they get from parents, professors, and professional development experts to try to bring their career dreams to life. That's what one up-and-coming corporate leader called it when I asked whom she turns to for career and work guidance. She isn't aware of any online resource, mentor, or personal contact who could provide relevant guidance like I received during my early years of employment. She has to pull together various resources that offer the right contextual insight to guide her to the path she wants. But it shouldn't have to be that way.

Ever since I learned those hard lessons early on, I've wanted to understand the "business of work"—the who, what, when, where, and why that makes people and the companies they work for thrive or fall back. Having been a strategist, marketer, and market researcher, I now innately look for the factors that determine success and failure. What holds people back? What gets people stuck? And what does it take to create positive momentum?

---

1   "Job Hopping," LiveCareer, September 25, 2020, www.livecareer.com/resources/special-reports/job-hopping.

What motivates me is helping others develop their own career trajectory, a task that is more complex than ever. Because you may not have anyone to help you. Early in my career, I built a village of mentors, friends, and family who supported me along the way. That village brought me through the hard times. Difficult as the 1990s and early 2000s were for anyone trying to find their way, no employment circumstances in my living memory compare to the challenges our eighteen- through thirty-five-year-olds face today.

The New World of Work

At the time of this writing, we are in a pandemic economy. General trends that have reshaped the world of work have given way to sudden, irreversible transformations. In the wake are left both seasoned professionals and young leaders without clear direction or useful advice. Sure, there's plenty of advice. But the guidance that established professionals, mentors, and employers can offer Generations Y and Z only works in a world that no longer exists.

Other books already discuss the what, when, how, and why of those changes in the finest detail. This book is not one of them. Instead, this book aims to briefly review where we, the collective global workforce, are in order to answer: *Now what?*

The more we understand the business of work, how that has changed, and its impact on us personally and professionally, the better equipped we are to handle its continual evolution, now and in the future.

That said, I doubt you need a two-hour PBS documentary to recognize that macro factors are different than they were a generation ago. The comparisons could not be starker. The median work environment has gone . . .

- from narrow, specialized work to hybrid work and broad tools
- from siloed, cubicled organizations to matrixed teams who collaborate remotely

- from identifying with the company you work for to believing in their mission
- from aspiring to work for name brands to looking for the exact "right fit"
- from company status reflecting on employees to employee success reflecting on the company
- from a small set of tools to complete one project to nearly infinite tools to switch between and multiple projects to manage
- from rigid "stay in your lane" structure that discourages entrepreneurialism to individual autonomy
- from separate work and home life to perpetual intertwinement, especially during and after COVID-19—we are always "on" and connected to work
- from sequential processes to the agile, "A/B test" approach to getting things done
- from narrow individualistic goals like stability and wealth creation to long-term impactful desires like purpose and passion

Overall, there is a convergence of work and life, digital and physical, profit and purpose, career and passion. This is markedly different from the clear separation between these elements in previous generations. What the next generation wants out of work is not singular or linear but multimodal and multidimensional. Today's rising business leaders have a strong need for meaning. This helps explain why staying the course at one job or with one project is no longer the norm. Rather, growth comes through testing, learning, and pivoting into work that has greater noticeable impact professionally *and* personally. For many, everything is tied to some higher order meaning. Their personal "why" needs to integrate with their identity and how they approach work and life.

No longer is there this rigidity and hierarchy to the way we work. Rather, there is a democratization of work that has led to new approaches, models, attitudes, and expectations that upend traditional structures—like the one I learned to work my way through throughout my career.

Every shift brings opportunities and requires adjustments. For example, professionals who did not embrace new technologies saw their value as employees plummet. Those who leverage tech to get more, higher-value work done in less time advance in their careers.

If it's obvious that more freedom, more options, and more paths to success are unmistakably good, what is the problem?

That freedom, those options, and all those paths to success mean little if you don't know how to identify, experience, leverage, or follow them. What is freedom if it feels inaccessible? If there are so many options, then which are right for you? Which paths to success lead you to your desired destination? In theory, we know anyone can be an expert in anything by googling a subject and studying toward mastery all on their own. But again, access does not in and of itself mean outcome if there is not practical guidance.

Work has changed, and nobody is telling the next generation what to do about it. What it even means to "have a career" is so difficult to define, there is no longer one right answer. And *that* simple realization points us toward the answer. As *New York Times* best-selling author and modern Stoic Ryan Holiday says, "The obstacle is the way." Basically, there is no right or wrong way to find fulfilling work, grow your career, and fund your personal dreams. That is the secret to doing it all and having it all. It is naive to believe otherwise. The new world of work is itself a manifestation of a universal shift in society at large—and in our collective and individual psyche. That shift is what I call **fluidity**.

Fluidity: The Philosophy of Being Water

I have a black belt in karate. I'm Chinese American. It's not surprising that I love Bruce Lee. You too have probably heard or read the martial arts legend's famous line, "Be water." Two words, great depth. It's useful advice for martial arts practitioners whose fluid movements allow them to adapt to any opponent. In the context of a culture's changing values, beliefs, and norms, the quote carries fresh insight.

Don't get set into one form, adapt it and build your own, and let it grow, be like water. Empty your mind, be form-less, shapeless—like water. Now you put water in a cup, it becomes the cup; You put water into a bottle it becomes the bottle; You put it in a teapot it becomes the teapot. Now water can flow or it can crash. Be water, my friend.[2]

Lee himself is an example of fluidity, as he learned Wing Chun but later adopted other martial arts philosophies into his own martial arts mashup style and philosophy, which he called *Jeet Kune Do*, "The Way of the Intercepting Fist."

It wouldn't surprise me if Lee's analogy reminds you of "flow state," the everyday term used to describe that feeling when your mental, emotional, and physical energy are directed toward a singular activity or purpose to the exclusion of all else. Yet flow state feels effortless. Because it is—like water.

One of the core tenets behind [Bruce Lee's physical study of martial arts] is that there are no separate movements of offense and defense, they can happen simultaneously and flow quickly together. This is an idea that can be applied to our movements in life, bridging the gap between happenings so that you can flow easier from one thing to the next.

If we collapse the space between two separate movements, the result is flow—and when you're in flow everything moves more quickly and smoothly without much effort.

Forward movement becomes quicker when you don't force or strain—you adapt and adjust in real-time, all the time.

Gentleness and Firmness also work together to bridge the gap. There is an interplay of movement between them, they are not separate motions or ideas.[3]

---

2   "Bruce Lee," Wikiquote, November 18, 2020, https://en.wikiquote.org/wiki/Bruce_Lee.

3   Shannon Lee, "#62: True Flow: Bridging the Gap," September 7, 2017, in *The Bruce Lee Podcast*, https://brucelee.com/podcast-blog/2017/9/6/62-true-flow-bridging-the-gap.

This is the flow state of mind, and we all have it to a certain extent. Because we don't really have a choice. Fluidity is everywhere.

Fluidity (noun)
1: the quality or state of being fluid
2: the physical property of a substance that enables it to flow[4]

It's the shift from linearity to fluidity, siloed to collaborative, singular to multiple, right and wrong to relative. Consider how our understanding of personal identity has changed. Nonbinary. Gender neutral. Gender fluid. Not two ways to be—male or female—but several. Or none. Some days an individual identifies one way. The next it's totally different. Fluidity.

Which brings us to race. Our populations include a growing percentage of biracial and multiracial children.[5] My kids are biracial and switch identities depending on the context. They switch racial identities based on the environment. Sometimes they say, "Because we're Chinese, we're really good at math." Other times they say, "I can't say that because I'm white." Other parents I know with bi- or multiracial children have shared similar anecdotes. They use labels loosely in social encounters but otherwise have no practical use for them.

In most households, no longer are there separate roles of breadwinner and homemaker. Two (or more or fewer) partners reverse roles. Women now earn more than men in almost a quarter of couples.[6] Many men have adopted caregiver roles (e.g., stay-at-home dads). To keep up with demands of blurred work-life responsibilities, women constantly context-switch between mom, wife, worker, etc. Within the role of

---

4   "Fluidity," Merriam-Webster, accessed December 29, 2020, www.merriam-webster.com/dictionary/fluidity.

5   Marna Clowney-Robinson, Karen Downing, Darlene Nichols, and Helen Look, "Mixed-Race Matters: The Growing Multiracial Population and its Implications for Libraries," PIPEline, June 5, 2019, https://apps.lib.umich.edu/blogs/pipeline/mixed-race-matters-growing-multiracial-population-and-its-implications-libraries.

6   Claire Cain Miller, "When Wives Earn More Than Husbands, Neither Partner Likes to Admit It," TheUpshot, *New York Times*, July 17, 2018, www.nytimes.com/2018/07/17/upshot/when-wives-earn-more-than-husbands-neither-like-to-admit-it.html#:~:text=Today%2C%20women%20earn%20more%20than,Center%20survey%20found%20last%20year.

---

parent, additional fluidity is expected. Mothers are often project managers for their homes, for the kids, for their friends, for their spouses, for aging parents, and for work. The morning I wrote this chapter, I was a technical support specialist for my kids' web-based class while working on a client's project in my home office. My own mother did not have to blur this many roles at once.

More and more men have taken on multiple roles, supporting partners as equals and contributing to household chores. This is especially true for those who work from a home office, freelance or work part-time, or run their own venture.

Speaking of business, products like men's makeup, androgynous clothing, football equipment for girls, and dolls for boys show that the traditionally accepted binary lines are blurred. Maybe they're not straight, rigid lines at all, but living streams. Water.

In the same way, personal fluidity is seeping into our careers. After all, work-life separation is a thing of the past. Because people are thinking differently, we're executing differently. Popular human resources blog *Workology* correctly points out how we no longer identify with a title and job description but move from projects and switch teams so the company can get the most out of our experience, knowledge, and capabilities "in partnership and considerations of the person's curiosity and competence."[7] It only makes sense that organizational and individual interests align. In a national study on job satisfaction, 95 percent of respondents said that feeling like they can "be themselves" at work directly impacts their engagement. And 75 percent said that working for someone who listens to their concerns and meets their concerns is essential to retention.[8] The professional and the personal, mashed up.

This job fluidity flows right into workplace fluidity, *Workology* notes. With rigid siloes washed away, replaced by ever-changing

---

7   SHRM Bloggers, "Embracing Workforce Fluidity," *Workology*, December 28, 2016, https://workology.com/embracing-workforce-fluidity-in-2017/.

8   "Employee Engagement and Satisfaction Research Results," Ultimate Software, accessed December 29, 2020, www.ultimatesoftware.com/Contact/employee-satis-faction-research-whitepaper?from=homepagelist.

industry stability, marketplace demands, and even organizational structure, many companies now have "alternative collaborative constructs, the absence of formal organization structures, and even team-based hiring and compensation."[9]

Here are the implications. People have already begun to redesign business processes to reflect their flexible way of thinking and adaptable way of working, i.e., always ready to pivot. We're shifting from gate-kept decision-making to being inclusive and collaborative. Agile development approaches and the lean start-up model where you're in a perpetual beta state, always looking to improve, is the new norm. Here again personal and professional fluidity flow into one another. Professional development and entertainment consumption both involve seamless platform switching (e.g., book to audiobook, podcast to video, text to voice). Anything we want to know, we google. It's a bootstrapped education!

We want a certain setup in our lives, so businesses and the overall marketplace are catering to us. For example, the gig economy is the product of people wanting their work to fit around their lives. By jumping from job to job, skilled workers are expanding their skills. They're forming talent breadth *and* depth like never before. They're creating their own mashup in many ways. Add to this dynamic the globalization of talent. Companies can access the best talent not only in their local area but also the world. No one company really "owns" the best workers in a certain discipline anymore either. For example, top computer programmers can hop from big tech start-up to big tech corporation or go freelance and work for them all. This leads to increased competition—and the need to keep up. Companies must do the same. Adapt, iterate, evolve, or die. Speed to market—or expediency to whatever the goal—is essential.

A downstream effect is how companies source the people who work for them. As resources allow and demand determines, they scale their workforce up or down—contract, freelancer, part-time, full-time,

---

9   SHRM Bloggers, "Embracing Workforce Fluidity," *Workology*, December 28, 2016, https://workology.com/embracing-workforce-fluidity-in-2017/.

consultant, local, regional, national, global, you name it. Meanwhile, these organizations' forward-thinking leaders are expanding the company mission from shareholder value and profit first to profits, people, and the planet. Yet another result of workplace fluidity is providing workers location independence (even before COVID-19) and office hour flexibility. Workers can get the job done any time and place instead of between 8:00 a.m. and 5:00 p.m. I expect that in the very near future, organizations will work to empower their employees and contractors to prioritize their mental health. We will recognize the importance of addressing and integrating mental health and physical well-being into the idea of "work" itself. Well people perform well.

Do you see it now? Fluidity is the new way at home, at work . . . everywhere. It's the secret to harmonious relationships, an identity that feels authentic, and a satisfying career that provides for your financial goals and funds your personal ambitions. Again, there are no boundaries between the personal and the professional except in the advice we give most leaders and professionals.

Which brings us full circle—what are you supposed to do? To know that fluidity is our new normal is one thing; to leverage that awareness to help you and your career (or business) thrive is another. Society has not established a new "common sense" standard for the ideal career. When the ideal career for you is one that has never existed in that exact way, shape, and form before, there is nowhere to go for help.

As a result, there is a void to fill. That's probably the reason you picked up this book in the first place. You have professional ambitions and personal goals but haven't yet found the step-by-step advice you've been seeking.

I would like to take this moment to say thank you. The desire to share valuable lessons from others nontraditional career journeys and being able to pay it forward to the next generation of leaders searching for their North Star inspired me to write in the first place.

With this book, you are receiving my humble attempt at the first curriculum for fluid career design—the mindset, management philosophy, and operational approach that accurately takes our new, fluid normal into account before dispensing career guidance to better your future. This book explores these areas of work fluidity to create sound, actionable advice for anyone who seeks to move ahead in their career in today's dynamic, tech-enabled business ecosystem. But the future of work—the future of *your* work—is more than technology. Yes, advancements and breakthroughs change the way we want and need to work in the future. Think an artificially intelligent chatbot indistinguishable from a human assistant, or an augmented reality home office that makes a kitchen laptop setup look like the company boardroom. I'll not add to these predictions because I see an issue going unaddressed.

The Future Is Fluid

The future of work is human and individualistic. Thus, generational dynamics influence everything. Companies are made up of individuals, and individuals from every living generation have a unique and valuable way to look at the world of work. No one can change the environment in which they grew up and how it shaped their attitudes, behaviors, and motivators.

How do different generations' different ways of thinking, feeling, and operating in life translate to a new approach to career development and to work itself? Technology has caused notable shifts, but with so many digitally native people entering the workforce, it seems less important to focus on tech and more on what those generational differences mean for the way individuals and companies use the tech. To me, technology is becoming like electricity—it's ubiquitous to the point of invisibility. Digital touches every aspect of our day. It's just the way it is now.

In studying generational behavior, I've noticed a shift in work mentality driven by new soon-to-be-dominant generations who are open, collaborative, and entrepreneurial relative to generations past. They don't see divisions and hard lines between what you can and cannot do. It's this *and* that, not this *or* that. They don't want to be boxed in. They want to do multiple things. There aren't limitations, and they feel they can be good at anything. This way of thinking has not been prevalent in prior generations because it was not widely known it was an option. Technology that has made fluidity possible did not exist.

Because of the next generations' desire to constantly test, learn, iterate, optimize, pivot, and do it again to find what really floats their boat—they are in essence thinking and operating fluidly. And they are comfortable with it. By trying many things, they are progressing toward an ideal career "mashup" that fits all the goals (or objectives) they consciously (or even subconsciously) want to fulfill. While they don't know what that mashup looks like, it certainly doesn't seem to be something offered in most work environments today.

This is why fluid thinking (and doing) and fluid career building are essential. Because we must think and do differently in our changing world. Change (and now uncertainty) is constant. My hope is that the insights, perspectives, and recommendations I've included will help you better navigate your work life so you can reach your full potential.

CHAPTER 1

Be Your Own CEO—
Because You Have To

Times have changed. What once worked to build a reliable career, make a great living, and feel good about your impact on the world has changed. Our parents told us to go to a good school, graduate with respectable grades, get a stable job at a big company, work hard to move up, go to graduate school, reach the top, and retire comfortably. That's not a true path in the new economy.

Recently, I spoke with my friend Steve to discuss why. Steve is a CIO of a leading global investment banking, securities, and investment firm. He is also executive director of a nonprofit I support. As often happens during chitchat with work friends, our families came up.

"The other day, my son told me, 'Dad, I want to be a CEO someday,'" Steve said. "I don't want my son to become CEO of some big company," he said. "I actually directed him away from joining any large established corporations. 'Be your own CEO,' I told him. 'Find a need in this world and fill it. Make a new company. Employ good, smart people. Build them up so they're as successful as you. Then find ways to give back.'"

"That floors me," I said. "Not because I disagree with you. I *do* agree. I'm just . . . surprised. The fact that an executive of a thirty-billion-dollar company prefers their child to take a different approach is noteworthy."

"It is," Steve said. "Look, I've seen a career path and mindset shift across the three generations I've worked with. Older generations work for a company and then move from company to company. Yet they're not totally fulfilled on a personal level from their work. They have been limited in their career advancement. That's just the way it was. Now, we've got kids in their early twenties who are working on multiple projects with a side hustle on top of that. Usually, it's something they're passionate about that could turn into a real business."

"I've noticed that about the young professionals I mentor as well," I said. "Those who do take their side gig full-time are happier."

"Exactly," Steve said. "Even though I've been successful through linear progression, that's not considered success anymore. It's not about becoming a VP, managing director, or president of a company. Success is about having a bigger social impact. And it's about happiness. People who take control of their destiny want to give back."

"It sounds like you're saying that success means a lot of things now," I said. "It's not only about career advancement through big promotions and high salaries. Success isn't one-dimensional anymore."

"I want my son to establish his own success milestones rather than leap onto a traditional corporate path. When you make your own company . . . when you achieve personal success and cultivate people instead of just gathering wealth, you create jobs and build up your community. Making your own destiny means naturally contributing great things to society."

Steve went on to tell me how he is encouraging his son, even as a teenager, to thrive under his own banner instead of boxing himself in. At sixteen years old, his son has an internship with Stanford University, is entering an entrepreneurial start-up program at another university, and started his own clean energy tech start-up. All of his own volition. He already thinks and operates very differently than generations before him.

"My son even said, 'I'm going to start at the top, and I'm going to create the bottom,'" Steve added. "And I agree."

I was surprised by how progressive Steve's thinking was around career development and progression given that he was a successful by-product of the corporate linear path. Even his definition of success was multifaceted, not the singular view that many of us had focused on, which was wealth creation.

Because Steve has been successful on his path, I assumed he would give advice for everyone to follow that track. But working in tech, he's been privy to a different way of thinking. Banking is traditional, but tech changes constantly.

Broadly speaking, every parent wants their children to shoot for stability and purpose. In the past, that often led the last generation to tell the next generation to follow them on the same paths that they believed in and observed to work. To shoot for companies with name recognition. They would want them to have the best chance.

"It's wonderful that you're making him aware of the world so young. When you're your own CEO, you have a voice and you have a choice. You can promote yourself. You have a seat at the table. You can respect your own ability to contribute."

"That's true, but that's not all," Steve said. "We don't live in a world anymore where a Fortune 500 job is always the best job. Taking risks is the right thing to do now, and failure is a good thing. Success isn't single variable anymore. We used to focus on wealth creation, but now higher-paying jobs come with trade-offs. Reaching the C-suite level, great, you're successful, but what have you really done? You made your company rich, but if you are successful by creating your own company, you've done other things for society. That's real success because you've created something and you can control your own destiny."

"Exactly what I've been noticing as well," I said. "Career goals are now mashups. People are aligning passion, purpose, and making a living into one. Your son is already doing that, it sounds like. He's using all of his experiences to build his skills and chart his own path."

"Exactly," Steve said. "A decade ago, rising to CEO of a large investment bank marked the pinnacle of corporate and personal success. Not anymore. Everything is different now. When you're your own CEO, you always have a job. You may not always get paid, but you always have work to do that could get you paid."

"There's a word that describes the career journey your son is already taking. It's the same journey everyone is on now, whether they know it or not. Not because they want to take it, but because they have to."

"What word is that?"

I smiled.

"Fluidity."

The Only Constant Is Change

So how did we come to live in a world where an investment bank CIO tells his son to seek a different career path?

On my podcast *Strategic Momentum*, I've interviewed over one hundred established career professionals and rising industry stars. The ages of my guests range from their early twenties to fifty and above. Industries and backgrounds are as diverse as you could hope for, including progressive entrepreneurs, accomplished executives, leading psychologists, and best-selling authors. Regardless of career, these guests' stories all share one common thread: pivoting, testing, learning, and evolving throughout their journey was what led them to where they are today. Many had experience in one field or industry that they were able to leverage to help them in a different one. To create that new role, they had to be fluid—they had no guidebook to follow because what they were building had not yet been created by anyone else before.

By one popular estimate, 65 percent of children entering primary school today will ultimately end up working in completely new job types that don't yet exist. In such a rapidly evolving employment landscape, the ability to anticipate and prepare for future skills requirements, job content, and the aggregate effect on employment is increasingly critical for businesses, governments, and individuals in order to fully seize the opportunities presented by these trends—and to mitigate undesirable outcomes. In short, it's up to them to find their flow.

The model of career progression and growth used to be linear. Job opportunities coupled with additional education advanced workers from one level, one department, one pay grade to the next until they reached C-level or their profession's equivalent (or retirement). But avalanches of change, some shifts slow and others sudden, demolished everything that was. As we look toward the middle of the twenty-first century, the career landscape before us is no longer a mountain with ever-higher peaks. It's a land of slopes, cliffs, valleys, hills, and hollows. In nature, the substance best suited for these environments is flexible. Agile. Fluid.

Water.

We may wish for the return of a rigid, hierarchical structure with a You Have Arrived destination clearly marked. But just as movements of ice and snow irreparably transform the earth, so change has done away with the old pathways to success. New technologies, social change, generational shifts, and the simple passage of time have brought us a world where the fluid way is the best way. To understand your place in it, let's start with how we got here.

Automated Change

Automation is streamlining repetitive processes that people used to do, from assembly line labor in decades past to tedious manual tasks like audio recording transcription. Automation's benefit is efficiency, but its downside is the obsolescence of many careers. With technology and machines taking on more repetitive tasks and people's work becoming less routine, the jobs themselves are forced to evolve—or go extinct. McKinsey & Company predicts that eight hundred million jobs will be automated away by 2030.

Jobs considered automation proof are those that are multidisciplinary, creative, and data and information driven. These jobs are also interpersonal. There is a recognition that automation is killing opportunities for human-to-human communication. Thus, there is movement to ensure touches of humanity even in the virtual world. When the competition is all digital, the new offer that includes real people has a distinct advantage.[10]

That's not all we can thank automation and its close kin artificial intelligence (AI) for. AI has permanently changed what it means to have a job. The 2019 Deloitte Global Human Capital Trends introduced the word *superjob* into the workplace lexicon. As AI and other technologies remove more and more tasks from the typical employee's work, that individual's ability to engage in higher-level activities increases in value. Soft skills like persuasion, data interpretation, active listening, problem-solving, negotiation, de-escalation, empathy, collaboration, and teamwork become as essential to any job as the job itself is to the organization. Deloitte points out that the highest-in-demand and highest-paying jobs over the next decade will be these "hybrid jobs" that mash up technical skills and soft skills.

But the concept of superjobs takes this shift one step further.

> Superjobs require the breadth of technical and soft skills that hybrid jobs do—but also combine parts of different traditional jobs into integrated roles that leverage the significant productivity and efficiency gains that can arise when people work with smart machines, data, and algorithms.[11]

In short, increased automation together with the growing desire to bring our whole human selves to work (and to each transaction) is "forcing organizations to create more flexible and evolving, less rigidly defined positions and roles."[12] Again, evolve or die.

---

10   James Manyika, Susan Lund, Michael Chui, Jacques Bughin, Jonathan Woetzel, Parul Batra, Ryan Ko, and Saurabh Sanghvi, "Jobs Lost, Jobs Gained: What the Future of Work Will Mean for Jobs, Skills, and Wages," McKinsey & Company, November 2, 2017, www.mckinsey.com/featured-insights/future-of-work/jobs-lost-jobs-gained-what-the-future-of-work-will-mean-for-jobs-skills-and-wages.

11   "Leading the Social Enterprise: Reinvent with a Human Focus. 2019 Deloitte Global Human Capital Trends," Deloitte, accessed December 30, 2020, www2.deloitte.com/content/dam/insights/us/articles/5136_HC-Trends-2019/DI_HC-Trends-2019.pdf.

12   Ibid.

Remote Change

Another way the world of work has changed is where people work, which then impacts when they work. Because you can do your work from anywhere, this naturally bleeds into the fact that you can also do work at different times of the day.

Prior to COVID-19, the common yet misguided belief was that employees wouldn't be productive (or trustworthy) enough to do the work when they said they would. The implication was that it would be harder to manage them versus their onsite peers. That hasn't proven to be the case.

In fact, remote work creates opportunities to find the best talent anywhere in the country—and the world.

Location and time zones no longer matter. There can even be efficiencies with teams working in different time zones as they could be getting work done faster (while you are sleeping they are working, and vice versa). This has enabled a fluid ecosystem where a company could hire the best workers from various regions without location-based obstacles.

During the coronavirus pandemic, many traditional corporate companies were forced to mass test remote work for the first time. Where executives had previously feared a productivity plunge, they instead gained workers with improved mental health, not the least reason being the end of stressful daily commutes.[13] Further, there were lower utility bills and downsized commercial real estate.[14]

---

13   Brie Weiler Reynolds, "The Mental Health Benefits of Remote and Flexible Work," Mental Health America, accessed December 30, 2020, www.mhanational. org/blog/mental-health-benefits-remote-and-flexible-work.

14   Jim Berry and Kathy Feucht, "2020 Commercial Real Estate Outlook," Deloitte, accessed December 30, 2020, www2.deloitte.com/us/en/insights/industry/ financial-services/commercial-real-estate-outlook.html.

Role Change

The continuous change and speed at which change is happening in business is impacting everyone at all levels. As a result, people and the teams they are a part of have to flex up, down, left, and right more dynamically than ever. You have to be adaptive and responsive. Being a utility player is now incredibly valuable versus being the position player that can't change or learn a new skill.

There's a need to move fluidly both horizontally and vertically across roles and the organization. It's being adaptive *and* responsive to the situation, the project, the people in your team, or even your leader. You now have to be a thinker and doer, player and coach, mom/dad and leader all at the same time—at any point in time.

And with organizations changing from more traditional siloed functional structures to ones with more open boundaries, the bleeding of the lines will be more common, creating a more fluid, dynamic group of employees that form around a problem or opportunity.

When I entered the workforce in the 1990s, clear lines were drawn as to who did what and which group owned what. Marketing personnel reported to marketing management, worked on marketing projects, and got promoted to higher positions in the marketing department. This allowed companies to keep work within a closed system where they maintained control and saved money. Marketing consisted of mostly full-time salaried professionals whose niche was marketing all their lives. The gig economy changed everything about this.

> Gig economy (*noun*):
> an environment in which temporary positions are common and organizations contract with independent workers for short-term engagements.[15]

In the gig economy, marketing can hire a graphic designer to create one graphic, collaborate with one agency on one advertising campaign,

---

15   "Definition: Gig Economy," TechTarget, accessed December 30, 2020, https://whatis.techtarget.com/definition/gig-economy.

and farm out communications tasks to a copywriter who exclusively writes copy for companies in that industry.

The Great Recession and easy-to-use platforms to hire qualified professionals on-demand together changed the way we think about careers and how companies leverage part-time gig workers, contractors, and retainer professionals. Companies are seeing the advantages of delegating specific functions that do not require the same managerial oversight as a full-time employee.

The gig economy works simply because the technology it's built on allows anyone to have a side hustle—and because many people need one. Freelancers have multiple jobs or projects where they could be wearing several hats depending on what their clients may want. And even a freelancer or contractor's role in a company could constantly morph depending on the needs and objectives.

Role change also means that with home life and work life blending, a woman may have to switch between being a leader of a project one minute to a mom trying to help her kids with virtual schoolwork the next. Those lines are now completely blurred, and the speed in which we need to context-switch between roles and responsibilities is now almost real time because life doesn't wait.

Really, "gig" is a misnomer because the implication is low-skilled, short-notice work that, once completed, requires little additional support. This could not be further from the truth. Over the past decade, gig work has expanded from entry-level skills such as data entry, transcription, and freelance blogging to now encompass sophisticated creative positions such as fractional (part-time) chief executive officer and other executive-level positions. For a few thousand dollars a month, start-ups with fewer than a dozen people are able to work with experienced executives who have several decades of experience in Fortune 500 companies to help them grow their businesses. This was simply not possible prior to the gig economy.

From the workers' perspective, the gig economy offers tremendous opportunity. Think of the fractional executive. If willing and able, they can fluidly manage multiple clients, earning several times their former corporate salary while de-risking their work by diversifying *who* they work with—a win-win situation. That explains why 87 percent of the nearly ten thousand global workers surveyed by ManpowerGroup say they want "NextGen Work," the term ManpowerGroup uses to describe the holistic experience that surrounds gig work.[16] It's about the money, and also it's not. ManpowerGroup puts it this way:

> NextGen Work allows people to supplement incomes over the short-term, provides freedom to explore different roles and develop in-demand skills to be more employable over the long-term. People can also control where, when and how they work, reducing stress and allowing flexibility for Life Work Balance.[17]

In fact, MBO partners, in their State of Independence, report that over the next five years, 54 percent of the US adult workforce will either be working or will have work as an independent at some point.[18]

Speed-to-Market Change

In business, the first mover advantage refers to the company or individual who "gets there first" with their product, offer, or idea. Bring your MVP—minimum viable product—to the market before anyone else shows up or be first to innovate, and the market's attention is yours. Think about the instant disruption in transportation and travel by Uber and Airbnb, respectively. The taxi and hotel industries were blindsided in a matter of months by people who were building on the fly. People who believe that perfect is the enemy of good. People who knew that time to market was essential.

---

16   "GigResponsibly: The Rise of NextGen Work," Manpower Group, accessed December 30, 2020, www.manpowergroup.com/workforce-insights/world-of-work/gig-responsibly-the-next-gen-at-work#:~:text=NextGen%20Work%20allows%20people%20to,flexibility%20for%20Life%20Work%20Balance.

17   Ibid.

18   "The State of Independence in America," MBO Partners, accessed December 30, 2020, www.mbopartners.com/state-of-independence/.

The Uber and Airbnb stories are not isolated incidents. We're all either Uber or the taxi company they displaced. Speed-to-market is a universal business goal at this point and is one of the top strategic priorities among executives in any company. Because if you aren't fast, your competitors will be and potentially beat you to the punch.

The first mover advantage also has implications for customer experience. The sooner you get out to market, the sooner you can find product-market fit. This is true for both products and for people. Customer interests and attention change quickly too. Your customers also expect it, as we live in an age of near-instant gratification. There's always the next big thing for them to explore.

Companies also are looking for flexible talent so that they can scale up and scale down dynamically as their needs change. This enables them to build that flexibility into their teams and organizations to help them get to market faster. Finding people who can learn, build, pivot, and adapt to a role that isn't 100 percent clearly defined at the start is necessary for any company who wants to win. Will you be one of them?

Scott Galit, CEO of financial services company Payoneer, attributes the market's speed change to the gig economy phenomenon.

> From the globalization of commerce, to the innovation economy, companies around the world are looking for flexible talent . . . Everything also really points to more technology-driven needs and there is not enough talent in the places people would like to hire and not as many businesses that are looking to hire permanently. They want more flexibility to try to be faster to market and retain more flexibility in how they build their teams and their organizations.[19]

Speed is more than how quickly you start. Our postrecession pandemic economy demands sustained urgency and punishes complacency. Companies in the past didn't need to course correct quickly because no one else could provide what they offered. If any new company came

---

19   Nicole Fallon, "The Growth of the Gig Economy: A Look at American Freelancers," Business News Daily, updated December 6, 2017, www.businessnewsdaily.com/10359-gig-economy-trends.html.

along that could offer even half the same value, they'd see the competition coming a mile off and could adjust at their leisure.

Globalization, the internet, and drastic events have changed the way companies think about strategy. Our networked on-demand economy forces even the largest and most secure companies to constantly reassess their own performance and find ways to more accurately hit ever-shifting targets. Small companies may rise overnight and steal an entire market space in a matter of months from the other side of the planet. Failing to respond to shifting customer needs and innovative competition is the path to bankruptcy. The best don't rest on their laurels; they push forward with a relentless desire to improve what they've already mastered. This is true for companies as well as for careers.

Mindset Change

Before COVID-19, the Great Recession, and the internet before that, fortunate people would land a position with a large company and hope to create a stable, long-term career there. The job itself became their identity. While occasional promotions and cost-of-living raises may have come down the pipeline, they simply had to do the job put in front of them.

That model is now obsolete. The new economy demands that every worker at every level on every team constantly improve their skill set and increase their knowledge. Refusing to adapt to change in our fast-paced world may result in you becoming too outdated to perform your job.

The modern emphasis on human actualization also leads employees to ask for more from their employer than strict cash. People don't just want a paycheck anymore. We want to work, but we also want to grow. We want to feel we're making strides as a person, becoming stronger, smarter, and happier. In addition to money, we want value and meaning, purpose and passion.

This fluid mindset also requires the acceptance of failure. Failure is a good thing because you will continually learn from failure. Fail fast to learn fast. This is the speed of business and life. It's not going to be "go big or go home" anymore. Test, measure, try again. When you embrace this in practice (like many high-growth start-ups do), you can achieve exponential growth in opportunities and income.

Predictability Change

Sudden and protracted events from terrorist attacks to pandemics have taught us to be certain about uncertainty. Most recently, the novel coronavirus forced leaders in all corners of society and at all levels of companies to stop asking, "What's going to change next year?" and start asking, "What's going to change in the next five minutes?"

Uncertainty is terrifying. Executives strive to create predictability. Investors are looking to minimize uncertainty because they want to balance risk and reward. It's a battle between, "We're not sure how bad it's going to get," versus "There's a lot of potential for amazing things here."

To survive COVID-19, employees, executives, and entire companies searched frantically for ways to create new safety measures and protections for employees, customers, and the public. This led to countless changes we are still only beginning to understand. This unpredictability is felt in every industry, in every company, and in every family. Only those willing to do what it takes to survive—no matter what—will be the ones who thrive on the other side.

Knowledge Change

Knowledge is useful, but knowledge alone is static. As customer demands change and technologies replace each other almost daily, companies require professionals who can learn and adapt at a moment's notice. Any employee, manager, or leader who thinks like a student and possesses an innate ability to "just figure it out" is an irreplaceable asset. This is especially true if the individual is self-guided, meaning they don't need costly training and hours of supervisor meetings. Yes, employees still need to know the fundamentals of their work, but knowledge is always under construction. The ideal worker is more like Wikipedia than a printed textbook—always updating, always revising, always expanding.

But that knowledge you have acquired isn't just learning about what it is. More importantly, it requires you to determine "so what?" and "now what?" It's about determining the implications of that knowledge and how to put that quickly into practice to make an impact. Memorizing facts and figures is not the valuable skill it once was. Within seconds, we can leverage free search engines to collect accurate, up-to-date information on just about any topic. The knowledge bar is now higher. The new marketable skill is not simply knowing who, what, where, when, or even how, it's being able to think through the "why" and the "so what." For example, if you're able to deduce *why* customer behavior is a certain way, you can apply that knowledge to company strategy to improve results. And if you understand what a new technology disruption means for your career, you're empowered to reposition yourself for success.

Career Development Change

Training and development programs are what everyone wants to continually level up and grow their skills. (And it's not just hard skills but also soft skills). Leaders expected that investment in their workforce would produce a return over time. This aligned closely with the traditional career, which was "predicated on the ideal of linear upward progression from job to job within a single organization with increasing status, responsibility and pay" with "the employer as the provider of stability and opportunities in exchange for the individual's effort and long-term commitment." In return, "career paths were designed to reward employee loyalty with upward mobility in terms of income and status."[20] Among these rewards was upskilling.

---

20   Sean Lyons, Linda Schweitzer, and Eddy S.W. Ng, "How Have Careers Changed? An Investigation of Changing Career Patterns across Four Generations," Journal of Managerial Psychology 30, no. 1 (2015): 8–21, https://doi.org/10.1108/JMP-07-2014-0210.

I joined the workforce out of grad school just as the sun was setting on corporate training and development programs. Leadership across the Fortune 500 and even small-business America believed in grooming their employees early in their career. That investment is now gone. In 1979, the average young professional received two and a half weeks of training per year. By 1995, that fell to eleven hours. In 2011, only 20 percent of employees received *any* on-the-job training in the previous five years in *any* jobs they'd worked during that time.[21]

Fluidity is both the cause and the effect, the challenge and the solution. According to Gallup, millennials change jobs three times more often than other generations. This turnover costs the US economy $30.5 billion per year. To many employers, the numbers don't make sense.[22] Why invest in someone who is likely to leave and add value to a competitor? As Peter Capelli, director of The Wharton School's Center for Human Resources, points out, companies really want people they don't have to train.[23]

Harvard Business Review recently noted that people with a college education are able to develop the skills that formal training did not provide. This is especially true for younger millennials and Generation Z, who tend to feel comfortable being self-taught and therefore "reskilling."[24] In years past, many organizations provided both training and development as well as mentorship—personalized, one-to-one

---

21   Peter Cappelli, "What Employers Really Want? Workers They Don't Have to Train," *Washington Post*, September 5, 2014, www.washingtonpost.com/news/on-leadership/wp/2014/09/05/what-employers-really-want-workers-they-dont-have-to-train.

22   Amy Adkins, "Millennials: The Job-Hopping Generation," Gallup, May 12, 2016, www.gallup.com/workplace/236474/millennials-job-hopping-generation.aspx.

23   Peter Cappelli, "What Employers Really Want? Workers They Don't Have to Train," *Washington Post*, September 5, 2014, www.washingtonpost.com/news/on-leadership/wp/2014/09/05/what-employers-really-want-workers-they-dont-have-to-train.

24   Marc Zao-Sanders and Kelly Palmer, "Why Even New Grads Need to Reskill for the Future," Harvard Business Review, September 26, 2019, https://hbr.org/2019/09/why-even-new-grads-need-to-reskill-for-the-future.

career guidance from someone who's "been there, done that." While it's known that there are positives to having a program like this in a company, for those who are choosing a different career path where they are freelancing or starting their own company, you don't have access to mentorship programs that have been proven to help career development and advancement. The opportunity to find those who could take you under their wing and teach you the ropes becomes even more elusive if you aren't part of a large or more established company.

Nowadays, it's not unusual for younger workers to pay for group mentorship, private career coaching, or nonacademic online courses to expand their knowledge base and improve and diversify their skills. Anyone still expecting to be spoon-fed career development from an employer will be disappointed—and left behind.

Process and Tool Change

This is about how decision and development processes were linear, gated, and sequential. You also had a small set of applications that you worked with because you were also more narrow and specialized in what you did. Now you may have to work with multiple applications, as your role could be broad versus deep and cut across various organizations (or, if you are a gig worker, various companies), to stay up to speed, manage the work, and even get ahead.

With the shift to agile processes and methodologies, organizations are able to move quickly to deliver products and services to the market. This has permeated all organizations, not just development teams, in needing to move fast.

Organizational Change

Because of this urgency change, there is a need to be more lean in the way organizations work. That means that a hierarchical organizational structure where there are clear roles and responsibilities is giving way to collaborative, team-based organizations. (It's the matrix or boundaryless orgs.)

The competitive pressures and technological breakthroughs are forcing organizations to structure themselves differently, which means the way you work with people will be different. Being constantly reforged won't necessarily be an anomaly but the norm.

One noticeable manifestation of this permanent shift will be what Gartner calls "extreme digital dexterity."

> Increasing demands for a more automated workplace has sparked the killer combo—people and technology. Proactive leaders must investigate how the regular use of AI, smart software and robots will invigorate work strategy, and to drive a competitive advantage, high performing employees should be encouraged to create and share AI tools or personalized portfolios of apps, tools and smart technology to raise the bar for extreme digital dexterity.[25]

The organization of the future (and present, really) embraces the latest technological innovations but more importantly nurtures an environment in which people can thrive using those technologies. Successful companies over the next decade are those that will enable their workforce through technology rather than minimize human involvement in favor of automated processes.

A publication of the United States General Services Administration expounds on the five ways organizations have and will change as a result of fluidity. Hierarchical structures are reduced so decisions can be made quicker, boundaries between teams and positions are broken so knowledge can be shared easily, agile teams replace bloated departments, and management commits to goals over rules.[26] As we've seen before, what

---

25   R.J. Cheremond, "6 Ways the Workplace Will Change in the Next 10 Years," Gartner, August 20, 2019, www.gartner.com/smarterwithgartner/6-ways-the-workplace-will-change-in-the-next-10-years/.

26   Judith Heerwagen, Kevin Kelly, and Kevin Kampschroer, "The Changing Nature of Organizations, Work, and Workplace," Whole Building Design Guide, updated October 5, 2016, www.wbdg.org/resources/changing-nature-organizations-work-and-workplace.

happens to companies happens to the people who work there. Those who can navigate the new organization will thrive in it.

Social Change

There is a continual trend toward companies thinking and operating in a more "conscious" way. Doing well by doing good isn't an anomaly anymore. In fact, CEOs of America's leading companies have shifted their mission from being about shareholder value first to a commitment around purpose—something all of us strive for personally. It's about leading their companies in a way that benefits all their stakeholders—employees, customers, communities—not just the shareholders.

Plus, corporate social responsibility is now an expectation among millennials, as what a company does will impact what this generation thinks about their brand and whether they will buy. Great examples of companies that have been doing it are Patagonia and Toms Shoes.

So company goals can't be profit *or* people *or* planet. It needs to be *and*, which is forcing companies to rethink the way they do business. To help codify this, the organization Business Roundtable published an open letter called "Statement on the Purpose of a Corporation," which incorporates employee investment, diversity and inclusion, ethical business practices, community support, and a fundamental commitment to human flourishing into what it means to be a corporation. The statement has been signed by the who's who of the Fortune 500, from Amazon's Jeff Bezos and Apple's Tim Cook to the chairpersons, founders, and presidents of the world's largest airlines, banks, consumer goods, and technology companies.

The New Worker

With all these changes, today's market has created a new breed of worker. These are not the cookie-cutter professionals of past ages. The modern professional defies labels and rejects boxes, instead favoring a variety of experiences to help shape their work lives into dynamic and meaningful careers that happen to have a paycheck attached.

Now that you understand the forces shaping your new environment, let's take a look at the people sharing space with you.

Job Hopping Is the New Advancement

Previous generations could work for the same company and find fulfillment in earning a living. Modern workers are looking for growth and new experiences. Even if the opportunity to work for the same company for their entire life presented itself, your peers, coworkers, and even your managers are unlikely to sit for too long in one place. People get the itch to move on and find new excitement in their professional lives.

Entertainment media producers understand this restless drive to experience something new. Video streaming companies present a million options at the press of a button so their customers can grab an interesting new show, binge it, and move on with a seamless experience. Optionality is the new normal.

Employment is shifting this way as well. Professionals talk about how their job makes them feel, what they're getting from their current position, and what field they want to try next in much the same language as they talk about digital media. People recognize their experiences are shaping their identity. Don't expect to stand still in a sea of people swimming around to find their next experience.

Purpose Is the New Pivot

Today's workers crave purpose. Employees and executives alike discuss passion as a driving force. If you have it, work seems effortless. If you don't, you'll wallow in misery.

With such a huge selection of opportunities, many people are learning from the ills of the boomer generation. Loyalty and long hours for stability in a job you're not fulfilled by isn't necessarily worth it. What millennials have learned is that toiling away like their parents did made them unhappy. Their parents told them, "Don't make the same mistakes we did."

But purpose as a driving force helps workers push harder through longer hours and tougher challenges. And smart executives harness this talk about passion and purpose in their mission statements as they roll out new procedures and campaigns to their employees.

Everyone is talking about purpose and passion. If you're just in this for a paycheck, you may struggle to connect with the people around you. Coworkers fascinated with passion may not network as enthusiastically with someone who has no desires.

Generational expert and president of Magnet Culture Cara Silletto has explored the emergent desire to find personal satisfaction in work. Millennials desire work-life balance, which to them means getting paid for work while feeling good about it—something that is yearned for across generations. The difference is that this is *demanded* by the younger members of the workforce.

What's critical, Cara pointed out, is the importance of understanding the "why" behind this new view of the world. Millennial children grew up in a world with options and an emphasis on having a voice—luxuries that weren't typically afforded to earlier generations. Early millennials grew accustomed to choosing their preferred food at mealtimes, receiving the gifts that they wanted for Christmas, and generally having equal input into family decisions. Their family dynamic was not a top-down hierarchy and a do-as-you're-told mentality. Millennials were told to find some type of personal benefit while still doing the best job they could. They were encouraged to follow their passion because life is short (which translated into the "you-only-live-once" mentality).

However, Cara explained that it's important to realize that these expectations are also shared by those in other generations and not just the millennial cohort, and thus they shouldn't be limited by age. It really is a cross-generational mindset, as others have shared these same desires but haven't had the power in numbers to affect change in the same way—until now.

Skills Matter More Than Titles

The accelerating pace of technological, demographic, and socio-economic disruption is transforming industries and business models, changing the skills that employers need and shortening the shelf life of employees' existing skill sets in the process. For example, technological disruptions such as robotics and machine learning—rather than completely replacing existing occupations and job categories—are likely to substitute specific tasks previously carried out as part of these jobs, freeing workers up to focus on new tasks and leading to rapidly changing core skill sets in these occupations.

There is a tremendous importance placed on job titles, but in today's job market, no title gives you a complete picture of what a role entails. In fact, the skills required to be successful may completely vary based on company and industry, so it's not always an apples-to-apples comparison.

Plus, titles reflecting certain roles today won't reflect roles that will emerge in the future based on new opportunities that didn't even exist before. It turns out that even LinkedIn and the World Economic Forum share that the best way to navigate this change and supply skills for employers is to describe it as an agglomeration of skills—they are essentially asking for the mashup.[27]

I choose the term *mashup* and not *portfolio career* for a specific reason: a mashup is more encompassing because it means you can build your hybrid of skills and interests into one role or into several roles that you work in parallel. We all want the flexibility to do either/or, after all.

Many authors can talk, but not all of them walk the walk they lay out for readers. For me, this book has already come alive at home. I teach this fluid yet systematic approach to my own family. For example, when my son was nine years old, I enrolled him in a free deejaying class just to see how he liked it. And he took to it like a natural. He built his

---

27   Allen Blue, "Does Your Job Title Matter Anymore?" World Economic Forum, January 18, 2016, www.weforum.org/agenda/2016/01/future-skills.

skills over the years and was recently starting to perform more regularly through gigs with his music school.

When COVID-19 hit, the gigs stopped and the practicing dwindled. With no clear idea as to when he would perform again, he became unmotivated and disengaged, even with the prodding of his DJ teacher, whom he loves.

I knew there was so much untapped potential that needed to be channeled in the right way. But the question was how to do so when there were no conventional ways to showcase what he loved to do. Performing to a crowd was what fueled him.

That's when I ran into a friend during an afternoon walk who happened to share an idea that would set wheels into motion. She was familiar with my son's DJ skills and said, "Hey, we were thinking just about him. Wouldn't it be fun for Dylan to do a dance party, a DJ dance party?"

Lightbulb moment. "Bingo, that's the idea. A virtual DJ dance party."

I pitched him the concept. "I'm going to give you a bunch of songs, and I want you to create a fun dance mix. You'll perform for a small group of people on Zoom to start. We'll see how it goes and take it from there."

He was definitely resistant at first. A virtual performance was a whole new thing for him, and fear initially got in the way. But he eventually got on board and started fleshing out his playlists. He blew me away, building a mashup of song combinations that I'd never even imagined. He hosted the virtual DJ party on Zoom, and the response was huge. People had so much fun that we collectively decided to do it again the next week, and the next. It became a weekly Friday night event for people to let off steam and enjoy themselves. His mixes appealed to folks across all age ranges from five to seventy-five, as he had this unique ability to seamlessly combine different genres and decades of music that seemingly wouldn't go together. His confidence not only grew by leaps and bounds but he also continually built these "hard" skills along with soft skills like communication and presentation week after week, getting more and more creative each time.

All of this culminated in him getting hired to do a virtual birthday party. And people loved it. We then pitched his middle school about doing an end-of-the-year virtual DJ dance party. His principal and his dean attended his weekly events, and so he got a loud yes. The party maxed out at a hundred guests within five minutes. At the end, the dean asked him, "Can you do another one for all the teachers?"

In November 2020, his middle school booked him for a virtual gig right before Thanksgiving. That party included 1,200 people. And he nailed it. His ability to be fluid had taken him to a whole new audience in the course of the year.

I include this story for two reasons. One, because I'm an extremely proud mother. And two, to illustrate my point that your skills can come from anywhere. You don't need three degrees and years of professional training to take your next step.

In creating a mashup as a DJ, you are creatively combining disparate songs that flow together with a common bassline (or other common thread) to create one overall mix. Just like with music, your skills and passions create that common thread among the different roles and industries that make up your career mix—even if they seem totally different on paper.

Successful career mashup skills aren't solely focused on hard skills. Soft skills are becoming more and more in demand, particularly in the virtual world we are continuing to live in. Humans need to connect, and those EQ skills—emotional intelligence—will be even more valuable than IQ.

Just as the ubiquitous jobs of the future do not yet exist, today's commonplace titles and roles may not exist in the future. That's why staying in the box and always in your lane won't work in rapidly shifting work environments. Many companies—certainly the progressive ones—are no longer looking to promote individuals who follow company procedures to the letter and never push beyond expectations. Leaders are on the lookout for out-of-the box, lane-switching thinkers eager to gain new knowledge, sharpen their skills, and advance in unforeseen new directions.

Your peers and your managers are on a quest to increase their own value to the company and to themselves. This means constantly fine-tuning their existing skills while developing whole new skill sets. Remember what I mentioned about people job hopping to find their next passion? Today's marketing manager may become tomorrow's celebrity DJ, and she's cultivating those skills now both during work and after hours.

Relying on your company to educate you and leaning on company support to embrace new roles means you'll fall miles behind your competition when your job gets automated, customer needs shift, or your company realizes they can pay an outside agent on the gig economy to get your job done.

The Career Mashup Is the New Job Security

Classic TV sitcoms portray the stereotypical worker clocking out from their shift to head home, drink beer, and watch television. Life revolves around a single professional job that never changes, and off-work time means pure relaxation and unplugging from thinking about money. What a quaint, outdated employment ideal.

Many professionals today don't look at one job, one career track, or one industry for their sole source of income. The side hustle is the new normal to make ends meet, have disposable income, or satisfy a passion. If the marketing manager is rocking DJ concerts on the weekends, Ted in accounting may start up a men's grooming company, and the woman who delivers your mail could be practicing for the next MMA tournament. As an aside, this mashup example shows how people can build up skills in an area that they aren't able to in school or in their full-time jobs.

Having a second (or third, or fourth) source of income decreases an employee's stress from insecure employment. When you're served notice that your current position will dissolve in six months, it helps to know you're only going to lose part of your income. People like to have options and backup plans, and multiple streams of income provide this security. Is your company job your only source of income? If your position disappeared tomorrow, would you still have food and shelter two weeks later?

Side hustles can improve one's skills in areas that they want to pursue outside of their full-time job, which they may eventually make into their main career. Built on skills like time management, leadership, and creativity, a side hustle is really a business at its core and as such is a way of channeling new skills, experiences, abilities, and interests.

Another aspect of the career mashup is not only about having various jobs but also that it could be an agglomeration (unique combination) of skills that could help you create an entirely new role in a company, making you incredibly valuable. This ties to the superjob point earlier from that Deloitte report. The mashup can happen in any way on a job level or on a macro career level. The main point is that you cannot be singularly threaded in any way anymore.

Secondary jobs also provide meaning and passion when the main job is lacking. Perhaps your day job feels like mindlessly pushing around papers for a heartless corporation. But you take those paychecks and dump them into your five-person nonprofit team that locates cheap and safe toys for underprivileged children. Or maybe Ted in accounting secretly hates the corporate world, but through his men's grooming company, he gets the chance to mentor young men who grew up without fathers.

Resting on a single job means you're vulnerable, and it means that job has to provide 100 percent of your professional purpose. Diversifying your income, skills, and time creates just as much resiliency as diversifying your stock portfolio.

Personal Brands Are the New Résumés

Today's professionals aren't just workers. We're a living brand. Employers will search your name and read the top results, check out your social media profiles, and make sure you aren't going to damage their company image with outrageous behavior. Everything you post online—every picture, word, like, and share—shapes your individual brand. Think about your personal brand. Right now, if someone searches your name, city, and state, what will they learn about you? What might your employer learn about you from your social media? Gary Vaynerchuk famously said, "Your personal brand is your reputation. And your reputation in perpetuity is the foundation of your career."[28]

Contrast the personal brand with the professional résumé. A résumé is the way you communicate your value to potential employers. A brand is the way someone perceives value. They are not the same. A brand is a continual pitch of the person or product that exists into perpetuity online, whereas a résumé is a static document that gets updated when its owner gets around to it or looks for a new job.

Personal branding is no different from a business strategy. Your brand defines who you are, what you do, and why you are different, which together create your unique positioning. You are a product on the web regardless of whether you have your own business, work in a company, or are a freelancer, so defining who you are, what you do, and why you're different becomes table stakes to set you apart from others. Just like marketing a product, service, or business, you need to do it to stand out. Your brand includes your cover letter and résumé, yes, but also your personal website, personal (or professional) blog, your social media profiles, and anything that shows up in search results when someone looks you up on a search engine.

Google is the new résumé. With the proliferation of social media and the gig economy, it's become essential to embrace personal branding because you have a personal brand whether you know it or not and

---

28   Caroline Castrilon, "How To Take Your Personal Brand To the Next Level," Forbes, October 30, 2019, www.forbes.com/sites/carolinecastrillon/2019/10/30/how-to-take-your-personal-brand-to-the-next-level/#:~:text=According%20to%20Gary%20Vaynerchuk%2C%20%E2%80%9CYour,in%20your%20field%20for%20help.

whether you like it or not. As Jeff Bezos says, "Your brand is what people say about you when you're not in the room."[29]

This is not a scare tactic, it's the truth. According to a recent Career-Builder survey, 70 percent of employers use social media to screen candidates during the hiring process, while 43 percent use it to monitor current employees' behavior.[30] Another reason personal branding is valuable is that the gig economy is not going away anytime soon. The average person switches jobs every two to three years; soon, freelance and contract workers will make up *half* the entire United States workforce.[31] Sooner than later, someone's going to google you and learn something about you (positive or negative), so it's critical to manage your online reputation and control your narrative. What do the search results say about you?

The Business of You

Since you picked up this book, it is safe to assume you are either not happy with what you are doing and where you are as a result, or you are happy but want to plan for the future. Either way, the path you've followed so far is now hazy at best and detrimental at worst. You need a new way forward, a new method to achieve success in this shifting world.

It could be that you've reached a life-changing decision to change your career focus. Maybe you're moving from accountant to outdoor

---

29   William Arruda, "The Most Damaging Myth about Branding," Forbes, September 6, 2016, www.forbes.com/sites/williamarruda/2016/09/06/the-most-damaging-myth-about-branding/#67c0ae7c5c4f.

30   "More Than Half of Employers Have Found Content on Social Media That Caused Them Not to Hire a Candidate, According to Recent CareerBuilder Survey," PR Newswire, August 9, 2018, www.prnewswire.com/news-releases/more-than-half-of-employers-have-found-content-on-social-media-that-caused-them-not-to-hire-a-candidate-according-to-recent-careerbuilder-survey-300694437.html.

31   Patrick Gillespie, "Intuit: Gig Economy is 34% of US Workforce," CNN Business, May 24, 2017, https://money.cnn.com/2017/05/24/news/economy/gig-economy-intuit/index.html.

adventure guide to find life purpose. Perhaps you've just opened a new company of your own in a desire to break out of the corporate box and reinvent yourself under a new banner.

Maybe, like my friend Steve, you're looking to provide a solid example to your children of how to survive and thrive in a global, mobile, ever-changing world that's reshaping what future opportunities look like. You picked up this book because you're looking to cultivate the mindset you need to flourish in the new economy.

The best place to start is by unraveling the tangled threads of your professional life. The reason unraveling your career is the place to start is because so many of us identify ourselves through the roles we play, especially our professional roles. That means getting to know yourself as a professional yet also recognizing what you may need or what holds you back personally. Those lives are no longer separate. You may ask questions like:

- Who am I? What makes me, me?
- What value do I provide?
- What skills do I possess?
- When someone hires me, what do I bring to the table?
- What past mindset biases have kept me stuck in the same boxes?
- What skills do I lack that I wish I had?
- Where in my professional life am I most frustrated?

Assessing yourself in an objective fashion allows you to lay the foundation to cultivate yourself in new ways. Finding out that your professional frustrations match up with your lack of skills in a certain area may create a remarkably easy path to making your life drastically easier. Similarly, discovering that you detest the field of work you're currently engaged in may inspire you to leap into an adjacent field with more meaning.

A key aspect of this process of change will be learning to take the lead versus being led. Do you have a goal, or are you aimlessly throwing experiences at the wall of your career to see what sticks? Reading this book means you're the kind of person who's unhappy with where others have been leading you—or where you may have led yourself. To fully leverage the knowledge you're going to learn in these pages, and to thrive in the new economy, you need to shift onto your front foot and get yourself going, not wait around for a manager, family, or friends to prompt you into action.

Bear in mind that the next step in your career is actually the next iteration of yourself. By launching into a new position or new field, you are redefining yourself. The goal is not to maintain a static existence but to find exciting new means of growth, new experiences, and new skills. Be excited for your career changes because they mean a better and more fulfilling life.

You're going to need to define or at least think about where you want to go and what you want to accomplish in the near term. There's no pathway forward when you have no destination in mind. Setting goals helps you figure out exactly how to advance and improve yourself. And these near-term goals should align to that vision of what you ultimately want to become. If your plan is to become CEO of your own smartphone app creation company, buying a restaurant may not be the best plan.

This book will press you to set many goals and objectives, not just one. These goals may be professional or personal, but in the end, they add up to the same thing: a more fulfilled you. Defining those targets will give you several paths to pursue, no matter where you're currently standing.

In the past, the two most common professional goals were usually wealth creation and role advancement in the same industry. But that's not going to be you. Defining your goals based on your who, what, when, where, and why will answer better questions than "How am I going to get a paycheck?"

It's about creating alignment between your goals, intentions, activities, and environment. Why do you work at this company or for these clients? What is your purpose professionally and personally? What is your passion? Are your interests, strengths, and skills aligned to what you are doing? Where can you leverage what you enjoy and where you perform well? And what should or could you be doing instead of what you are now?

If you are not yet satisfied with the answers that immediately spring to mind, not to worry. You'll soon learn how to fluidly align all aspects of your identity with the work you do and the environment in which you do it. To make that happen, however, you'll have to become your own CEO. And the fact is, you already are. Few know it.

What It Takes to Be Your Own CEO

You are going to control what seems uncontrollable. Here's how.

With there being constant change on a macro and micro level, being your own CEO, as my friend Steve said, is about finding ways to create some certainty in what fulfills you. If you continue to build on that, you can create certainty out of uncertainty but still have the ability to pivot.

The unknown is thrust in our faces every single day as we rush to catch up. Don't expect that to change. COVID-19 accelerated the changes, but many were already underway well before the virus. Changing back is not an option, because too many have tasted the freedom this decentralized economic world has brought. Fluidity is everywhere: at an individual, company, and market level.

No jobs are safe from these changes. A CEO with a track record of success may suddenly falter and never recover, while a younger manager with a fresh master's degree laps them with repeated successes. Contractors and consultants need to stay at the forefront of their fields or risk becoming entirely irrelevant.

In this rapidly changing business environment, failing to adapt makes you obsolete. Falling into thinking about your current career as your only option is professional suicide. The "golden handcuffs" trap keeps you stuck in place, but in the long term are you more eager for cash payouts or for life purpose? If staying with your employer for ten years gets you a nice cash bonus but stifles a hundred opportunities to grow by leaps and bounds, is the extra cash worth it?

The goal is not to remain loyal to any one company and rely upon those executives to push you into growth, or even to remain in one industry, but instead to practice self-management. Managing yourself as your own best resource ensures you are not devalued by unscrupulous employers or left with unrealized potential.

Change is constant in the new economic climate. More than ever before, uncertainty reigns supreme. Even experienced CEOs and industry leaders are struggling to forecast what changes will take place in the short term while trying to get a handle on the long term.

This can terrify you, or it can excite you. Because as rapidly as things change, we have the resources to keep up with shifting demands. Information is free and provided on demand. You can educate yourself with the smartphone in your purse or pocket in every spare moment.

Human labor used to be specialized and focused, like cogs fitting into a machine. Now you can reinvent yourself with a million new skills at your fingertips. If you want to break into a new field tomorrow, there are resources available right now to help you prepare enough to hit the ground running.

The generational shifts taking place are a battle between command and control versus individual agency. As the generations of the past, specifically the baby boomers and Generation X, give way to millennial executives, I expect this trend toward individual freedom to accelerate. Millennial bosses don't like ordering each other around any more than millennial employees enjoy being micromanaged. Neither side has much patience for people unwilling to educate themselves or who lack respect for the fluidity of our new environment.

To make the absolute most of your future, you're going to need to understand the way every topic in this chapter will impact your job, your company, and your skill set. You also need to know how this new fluid environment will shape what you want to do now and in the future, and what your next steps should be to realize your ultimate goal. The natural next question becomes, how do you take more control of your career and work life with less risk? There's a framework for that. And as you can probably guess, it's a fluid one.

CHAPTER 2

Fluidity and the Career Mashup

"What do you want to be when you grow up?"

We were all asked this question as children. The assumption baked into the question is that there is a stair-step approach to building your career and skills.

One label after the next, one box after the next. Somewhere between seventeen and twenty-three years old, we're expected to follow a logical and linear progression toward career advancement and even development. Within that profession, we can advance or specialize, but we don't stray off the trail. With time and luck, we climb to the top of the career ladder as family, friends, and colleagues applaud our diligent focus.

A convergence of factors has toppled over these boxes and ripped off the labels. As an undergrad, then graduate student, then young professional working my way up in corporate America, I felt this. I lived it. There was an unquestioned expectation to pick a path, stay the course, and progress upward. But I learned that I had to test, measure, and try my own thing to figure out what fit. That's how my journey began with a math degree but took me into market research and then marketing working in various industries. I started in one place but pivoted to another.

My story was uncommon in the 1990s, but not anymore. With the continuous technological advancements changing, the macro and micro dynamics of work and life evolving, coupled with a desire to align it to purpose and passion, we simply must find a different type of planning and way of thinking to blaze our own career trail into the unknown. Working for "the man," the top company with name recognition and all the perks, isn't going to cut it.

In the 2020s and beyond, building your professional identity around one primary industry, one dominant career path, and even one income means you're at a *dis*advantage. What happens when that industry gets disrupted; when that role is automated, downsized, or outsourced; or when that income stream dries up? When—not if.

By this point in the book, you're basically an expert on the why. We've learned about the events, disruptions, shifts, and innovations that have dismantled our "one-career-for-forty-years" system. The supreme question the rest of this book is dedicated to answering is: ***Now what?***

Let's answer that question with a question. Not to be ironic, but insightful. As children, we were asked what we wanted to do. That usually meant picking a specific path at some point and building on it. Now, as adults forced by change to navigate a fluid world, we must ask ourselves, **"What do I want to be so that I can fulfill my personal and professional goals?"** Bound up in this new question is the pursuit of passion and the development of new skills, both essential prerequisites for the new career.

To find our way in the new world of work, to "be water," we must be fluid in the way we think. This allows us to adapt both professionally and personally to "go with the flow" toward our personal and professional goals.

*That's all well and good, Connie, but **how**?*

A fair question. Well-meaning family members, teachers, and friends told us to hone in on a traditional career progression because that's what they knew. Professions like doctor and lawyer offer a clear-cut path to progression. What I'm not about to tell you is that you *must* go back to school. Additional education may or may not be a worthwhile investment for you personally. We'll dive further into continuing education soon. For now, what matters most is that there *is* a path to career success in the new, fluid world. And it's one that you get to create following a proven system based on the work and lives of those who've already made their own career mashups.

We're All Jennifer Lopez Now

J.Lo

You probably know her from her movies, her music, her moves, or all three. If you've followed Jennifer Lopez's career with even the occasional glance at grocery store tabloids, you may know Jennifer as a multipotentialite. She not only acts, sings, and dances, she is also a fashion designer, a movie and music producer, a fragrance entrepreneur, and a nonprofit foundation founder.

Some call Jennifer a "Renaissance woman." Others think she's crazy. But you and I know she's on to something. It's clear she has an interest in diverse industries across art, business, and activism, and she's found a way to "have it all." And she isn't the only public figure to do so.

If you follow the National Football League, you know the name Justin Tucker. He's the most accurate placekicker in NFL history, but have you heard the man sing?[32] While kicking his way into the record books, Justin has also received classical training, has studied opera, and has taken private voice lessons. Why? For Justin, the real question was, why not? While teachers told him he had to "pick one: music or sports," Justin chose both. Like most millennials, he has multiple interests and has found no good reason to *not* create his own career mashup.

Professional sports offer other real-life mashup examples. Justin's on-field opponent, Laurent Duvernay-Tardif, is both a lineman and a physician. During COVID-19, he took time away from offseason

---

32   "NFL Field Goal % Career Leaders (since 1938)," Pro Football Reference, www.pro-football-reference.com/leaders/fg_perc_career.htm.

training to serve long-term care patients, including those afflicted by the novel coronavirus, in his hometown, Montreal, Quebec. Why? Again, why not? The new world of work is not either-or, it's both-and.

Other notable career mashups we can model are found off the field and away from the stage. Arlan Hamilton is managing partner at Backstage Capital, where she exclusively invests in companies founded by women, people of color, and the LGBTQIA+ community. She is also the author of *It's About Damn Time*, published by Penguin Random House. Prior to business investing and authorship, Arlan ran her own magazine and managed Atlantic Records tours for recording artists.

Nick Loper, host of the award-winning podcast *The Side Hustle Show*, teaches listeners how to build job-free income streams. Nick himself has mashed up fifteen different projects, businesses, and products to form his own income confluence, all outside of a nine-to-five job.[33] These vary from advertising and copywriting to audiobook publishing and dividend investing. Nick's patchwork career approach is pretty simple. If he's interested in it, he tries to make money doing it.

Several professionals I know personally illustrate how diverse mashups can be. Yao Huang is a technology entrepreneur, venture capitalist, community builder, and comedian. Named by Forbes as one of eleven women at the center of New York's digital scene, by Beta Beat as one of 25 Women Driving New York's Tech Scene, and as one of TechWeek's 100 most influential people in tech, Yao believes in leveraging technological disruption and innovation such as virtual reality to scale social impact.[34,35,36]

---

33   Nick Loper, "303: The 15 Income Streams I'm Working on Right Now," Side Hustle Nation, updated October 4, 2018, www.sidehustlenation.com/income-streams/.

34   Julie Ruvolo, "The Rise of Hookup Mentorship among New York's Lady Digerati," Forbes, July 18, 2011, www.forbes.com/sites/julieruvolo/2011/07/18/to-the-entrepreneurially-minded-women-of-the-class-of-2011-new-york-welcomes-you/#3868e02b128b.

35   "Doing It for Themselves: 25 Women Driving New York's Tech Scene," *Observer*, June 6, 2011, https://observer.com/2011/06/doing-it-25-women-driving-new-yorks-tech-scene/.

36   Ashley Hoye, "Advice for Women in Tech from Leading Digital Entrepreneur Yao Huang," Young Leaders of the Americas Initiative, accessed December 31, 2020, https://ylai.state.gov/advice-women-tech-leading-digital-entrepreneur-yao-huang/.

She always knew she wanted to do many things and not have a career that would be narrowly defined. However, pressure from her parents to pursue a career in the medical field led Yao down the initial path to earn a doctorate in pharmacy. Thus she began her career in the pharmaceutical industry, where she was very successful in the way society deemed successful.

In Yao's own words, she "did really well, made lots of money. And as a young person, I hit everything you're supposed to do in our society. You're supposed to buy a house, supposed to buy fancy cars, supposed to go on fancy vacations, all that stuff. I was like an advertiser's dream."

But Yao eventually became bored and wanted more out of work and life. During that time of the first internet boom and even the first collapse, she was intrigued by the internet's potential and knew it was going to be something really meaningful in everyone's life and society. And she wanted to be involved in it. Thus her second career started as an entrepreneur when she founded her first tech company and garnered continued success on that front.

Another successful masher-upper is Joe Saul-Sehy, host of the number one financial advice podcast, *The Stacking Benjamins*. Joe was forty years old when the resignation of a mentor in the financial planning industry became a catalyst to change his own career trajectory. He chose to make a career pivot, taking him from being a successful financial planner and one of the select group of spokespeople for American Express to becoming an award-winning podcaster who leverages the science of play to build financial literacy among his listeners.

And this nonlinear journey has involved constantly testing and learning from his roles, cherry-picking the aspects he has a passion and aptitude for, and creating his voice by combining these skills and experiences.

Like many of our previous guests, the path to Joe's career post-college was launched through a fortunate stroke of serendipity. After graduating as an English major, he had "that horrible job you get right out of school that many of us get. Some people get the dream job. That wasn't me."

It was a friend who saw Joe's potential in the world of financial planning, as he was a planner himself. In fact, he said, "We normally don't hire people like you, but I think you'd be pretty good at this."

As someone who grew up in farm country and knew nothing about money, but who realized he had an engineering mentality, Joe leveraged these valuable assets as he began his successful sixteen-year career in financial planning. He owned his own franchise business while also becoming one of twelve media spokespeople for American Express and then later Ameriprise. His unique talent was that he could speak about money from a position of truly being that "Average Joe." Further, Joe's early days as a DJ in his teen years helped build those skills as an entrepreneur and entertainer, which he has continuously leveraged to this day.

Joe, Yao, Nick, J.Lo, and other successful career mashers have found that their knowledge and skills are easily transferred to adjacent fields—and even to completely different ones. Each new project is not a reinvention that replaces all that came before it. Rather, it's an addition. A supplement. A mashup.

It's not only diversity of income, it's diversity of skills and roles within a single job. It's a mashup within a job or a mashup of jobs. There is diversity within the job where there isn't one clear, defined role but also diversity of jobs. This makes you valuable in that nobody can do what you can do, which makes you safe from threats to that job and also to that income stream.

Think of your custom career as your business portfolio. You design your portfolio to hedge against risk and give you the ability to pivot immediately in multiple directions. Your career mashup simply diversifies your portfolio instead of relying on a sole source of income. This level of flexibility was once limited to those who were less skilled or had more service-oriented jobs, like a waiter jumping from one restaurant to the next or suddenly advancing to bartender. But today it is common among white-collar workers to have various freelance gigs, side hustles, and different sources of revenue. Instead of just running the marketing division at your company, you might also do executive coaching, advertising training, lead seminars on marketing, do marketing consulting for a variety of businesses, and so forth.

The goal is to play multiple roles, featuring a variety of functional and soft skills. For example, let's look at the next generation of chefs working in a restaurant. Jane is a master chef and a master at her craft. People come from other countries to sample the food she prepares. But Jane knows that, no matter how great her skill as a chef, the economy could tank her restaurant. So she studies every layer of her profession.

Jane learns what skills are crucial to starting chefs and what skills even seasoned chefs often lack. She obtains a teaching certificate that enables her to pick up a part-time job teaching other chefs at a culinary school. Jane also notices which of her tools are constantly breaking or identifies nonexistent utensils she wishes she could find in stores. She consults with a housewares company to create her own line of utensils, which feature her name on the handle. Now both chefs and household cooks know her name.

Jane teaches free cooking classes for low-income families to get them off fast food and help them start cooking more nutritious meals at home. While she doesn't receive financial compensation, she finds both purpose and passion in improving her community and the lives of vulnerable children who need better nutrition to thrive at school.

Jane plays multiple roles at the intersection of her interests and abilities. She's resilient against the economy ruining one restaurant, she's grown a wealth of experience, and she's built a network of powerful revenue streams. And each new role she steps into opens up a range of new options she can pivot to in the future.

To truly be fluid in your career, you need to know not only how to do your job but also the factors that go into doing your job well. If you learn these, you can teach them to others. Identifying problem areas in your field opens you up to consulting for businesses who support your current role. Finding the areas where your skills intersect with your passions allows you to find meaningful work to build your life satisfaction and achieve your personal goals.

Millions of millennials, Gen Xers, and now Generation Zs are finding themselves forced to innovate. Fortunately, what's been done before can be done again. What the well known, successful, and wealthy do has already been done by others. I would know; I've interviewed dozens of them on *Strategic Momentum*.

After studying the through lines of these career mashup stories, and working alongside corporate clients to uplevel their employees' skills, I've identified five fluid career components we all need to pass on our fluid journey toward our personal and professional goals. While our destinations may be different, what it takes to successfully navigate the new world of work is identical.

The Fluid Career System: The Five Components

Many people feel lost. Tips don't fix that. Systems do. Systems tell you what to do now, what to do next, and what to do after that. The bulk of this book teaches you a system to design your career mashup. Together, the five components will help you navigate your new flexible approach, understand your future of work, and learn to build powerful momentum in a fluid world. To do that, you'll learn to take control of your career path by building the business of you. Here are the five components to make that happen.

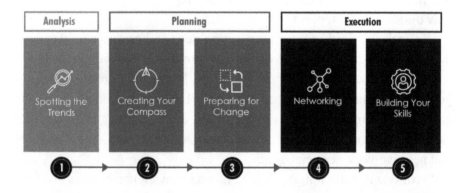

1. Spotting the Trends (Internally and Externally)

Charting your fluid course begins with knowing the lay of the land ahead of time. You may have heard the cliché about skating where the hockey puck is going, not where it is. That's what trendspotting enables you to do. For example, in the mid-1990s, I recognized that the future was web based, so I left packaged consumer goods for internet pioneer America Online. What trends do you need to be aware of? You'll learn not simply what they could be but how to identify them and how they could impact what you do now and in the future.

Sleuthing information about your industry, competitors, job function, and potential disruptions becomes more important with each passing year. But you need to know how to collect the right data *and* know what to do with it. If there's a new technology in your field, what are its implications on your role and skills? Are there shifting dynamics that affect your company, which then impact your position? What does that mean for you? And what do you do with your own evolving interests?

We'll answer these questions and more at the first component of the system.

2. Creating Your Compass

In the second component of the system, I'll show you how to leverage yourself as your own best product. Like technologies that disrupt, innovate, and add value, you, too, are a unique offer that will positively disrupt and valuably innovate in the way only *you* can. This is your mashup. You'll spin multiple personal and professional threads at once. Everything will operate in parallel. The question will be, where is everything going? What does your picture of success look like?

To answer those questions, you need a compass. You'll find out where you want to be based on what you learned about yourself in the first component and decide how to fill the gap between there . . . and here. The compass is the best metaphor because your journey will be directional rather than linear. Even as you shift and switch and pivot, you'll be doing so according to your own strategic plan. Yes, we'll actually create a strategic plan together as if you were a business. Which you are.

3. Preparing for Change

Millennials hit the job market expecting to find a clear pathway up the ladder and instead found a quagmire. The scarcity of full-time positions has forced many into multiple jobs to build a single livable income. Thus, many workers have had to reinvent themselves on the fly and diversify their income. With this book, you'll be prepared for such changes with a clear path to follow so you won't have to wing it the way the others were forced to.

This brings us to the fact that your career mashup will be unique. *It has never existed before*. That's quite a thought because it means there is no blueprint, no step-by-step instructions to plan your mashup. It might surprise you that this is good news because the flip side is . . . there are no limits, no ceiling, no maximum number of ways you can earn a living and feel good about it.

That does not mean dealing with change will be easy. Yet preparation for change is mental and emotional, not just operational. And there will be emotions. Fear. Anxiety. We will need to manage these throughout your journey, which is why the third component is entirely about doing so for the duration of your career.

This component is all about managing your fear, converting that energy into excitement, and developing your self-confidence so realize without a doubt that you know what you're doing. Even though you're doing what has never been done before—and even if people close to you believe that what you're doing cannot be done. You'll learn to release external pressure and overcome internal obstacles like self-doubt.

We'll explore more on how to prepare for change in the third component of the fluid career system.

4. Networking Toward Your Path

Fluidity does not simply apply to your career but also to your relationships along the way. Building your network—your village—is critical to getting where you want to go.

En masse, companies have shifted from strict hierarchies with siloed teams to matrix organizations or even boundaryless structures. If you work a nine-to-five, commit to supporting those who can affect your future. This includes anyone you report to, your department coworkers, and also professionals with your equivalent role on other teams. Understanding other functions and roles in your company besides yours allows you to truly support your team and identify new opportunities for growth.

To be fluid means to find comfort beyond your comfort zone. Professionals with deep connections outside their day-to-day projects and circles are at an incredible advantage. You can pivot to a new team within your department, into a different department, or even to a different role at another company if you ever want to or are forced to.

Not only will your new village make the introductions you need, they will point you to any skills or knowledge gaps you need to fill in order to stay fluid and open up even more opportunities in the future. Networking can help you create leads into areas that you want to pursue that may not even be in the field you are in now, but in one into which you want to pivot. You'll learn how to find and engage people who can better inform you on what to do and how to do it. Who knows, they might eventually be your advocate to support you in your journey. So it's aligning what you identified as your goals and objectives in the compass component and then finding the people who can actively help you to get there.

You are your own most valuable asset, and your village helps protect that value. Diversifying your relationships into a broad network of valuable relationships means you're ready for new challenges and will land on your feet when the unexpected pushes you off the path.

You're resilient, you're adaptive, and you're flexible. People don't just like you, they trust you.

You will learn the how-to of building your own high-value network during the fourth component.

5. Building Your Skills (Hard and Soft)

AngelList founder Naval Ravikant is known for popularizing the expression, "Play long-term games with long-term people."[37] The fifth and final component of your mashup system is acquisition of long-term skills. You're playing the long game, after all, so you need not only sustainable hard and soft skills but also the skill of gaining and developing more skills into the future. You're a living superjob, someone who is embracing "NextGen work." That will involve knowing where to pick up the necessary skills, when to practice them (at a job, in a side gig, etc.), and how to measure your progress so you can profit from them most.

There are two key skill-building concepts to remember when building your mashup. These apply to hard skills (e.g., coding) but also the growing importance and value of soft skills (e.g., communication). These two concepts are diversification and alignment.

Diversification means cultivating different talents and expertise drawn from your personal and professional experience. What you've done, what you've learned, and what you can do all weave together into a tapestry of ability. You want to be able to switch seamlessly from one role to the next. This also means keeping a mindset of continuous learning, constantly adding to your diversified pool of ability.

Alignment is the way complementary talents and skills from your diverse pool work together to open new avenues of income and opportunity. If you spend five years perfecting your chef skills while also working as a teacher's assistant, for example, you may decide to shift into an additional role as a part-time instructor at a culinary school.

---

37   Naval Ravikant, "Play Long-Term Games with Long-Term People," Naval, March 19, 2019, https://nav.al/long-term.

The goal of mashup careers is not necessarily to create wildly disparate roles. You're not setting out to become the world's first CEO, surgeon, and martial arts champion, for example. But starting as a surgeon and becoming the director at a surgical clinic by weaving together your administrative and medical expertise may be a smooth transition into an additional role with new opportunities.

Again, fluidity is not only about pursuing a variety of interests but also helping you see the connections and pivoting when necessary or when desired. What you're doing right now may not be needed tomorrow. This new system, which develops multitalented workers, helps companies in the end because it means they gain a wealth of new perspectives and options to grow the company.

Developing and augmenting your skills is more critical than ever before. Disruptions are increasing, not decreasing, as clever programmers discover new ways to streamline processes. Change is accelerating, and we can't possibly guess what tomorrow will bring. Technology has created a speed dynamic built on moving faster, speeding products to market, and staying competitive with faster service. The speed of your learning needs to change to match this frantic pace.

This means becoming a generalist. You don't have to be just one thing anymore! In the new world, you can't go deep without going broad too. Generalists can rise above the rest with a wide range of skills and can thrive when dropped into any raging storm. Companies used to focus on luring in the most talented specialists they could find and then finding a place for them later once they'd secured the geniuses. Today, specialists who cannot blend into new roles may become rigid liabilities who cost the company exorbitant salaries, where someone with half their knowledge may serve just as well while taking on additional duties. Creating your own mashup demonstrates a strong work ethic and a sharp mind for opportunity.

In this fifth and final component, you're going to learn the essential soft skills every business professional needs. You'll also learn how to best build those hard skills *you* need. You'll establish and add a portfolio of skills to your résumé, resulting in a comprehensive package where multiple jobs intersect.

Together, the five mashup components to manage the business of you will help you:

- push past the fear that holds you back and build your own confidence to move forward
- break the inertia from ideating, planning, and executing to reach your full growth potential
- align your interests, strengths, and skills to a plan for where you want to be
- spot the common threads between skills and experiences and how to leverage them
- expand your sustainable skill set
- recognize your growing success instead of getting frustrated when some areas seem weak
- connect more deeply with your current and future networks so you find a wealth of new opportunities
- create the product or service of you, leveraging yourself as your own best asset

In addition, this book will teach you how to be fluid, even across multiple career paths. The old single job was easy to track, as you just added up your status and salary and watched the line slope upward over the years. Now, with multiple different roles to track, you may have five different lines that wobble like sine waves. One job may tank, while another offers great success!

If you're feeling overwhelmed at the thought of finding your new place in the world of work, don't worry. I'll show you how to make sure you're actually improving. I'll teach what you need to be your own version of J.Lo. My promise to you is that I will not use anecdotes or unrealistic examples, but instead I'll supply pragmatic advice that is immediately actionable, habitual, and sustainable. Success is about having a process and making progress. How you build that process and how you get from strategy to execution is what comes next.

Are you ready to create your ideal career mashup? Good. Let's get started.

CHAPTER 3

Spotting the Trends (Internally and Externally)

Spotting (and Analyzing) the Trends

The human brain has evolved to recognize patterns. This is easiest to observe in small children, who like to test gravity above the kitchen floor at mealtime. This innate curiosity manifests in other, more practical ways as we grow. Each time we discover a predictable pattern, our brain goes to work figuring out how to leverage that predictability to our advantage.

But in the ever-changing business of work, spotting trends seems so much more complicated than My First Gravity Lesson: "Crackers fall when I drop them." There are so many shifting variables that people often get overwhelmed and give up. They settle for less than they're worth because they can't figure out their place amid disruption.

Learning to study, identify, and leverage patterns is key in the new world of work. So what's the key to keeping up with these trends? First, understand what information to gather from the volumes of information you could search for. Second, know what to do with that information once you collect it. In this chapter, you'll learn how best to gather and utilize information to get (and stay) ahead.

In academia, everything we do is grounded in the best available data, from publishing papers to determining which data we can trust in the first place. That's why trendspotting is more than knowledge. I knew that the future would be dominated by technology companies. But if I hadn't left my packaged consumer goods job to join such a company, what would have been the point? Ideas only have value when properly executed.

Trends, changes, and disruptions all *mean* something for you. When you figure out where the future of your industry or profession is headed (or the industry or profession you want to get into, for that matter), you need to ask yourself a serious question: Is that where you yourself want to be, or is somewhere else a better fit?

In 1998 during the dot-com boom, I read a little book called *Who Moved My Cheese?* It's the story of two humans and two mice searching a maze for cheese. I know, I know—in what world are animals and people trapped in a cheese maze? The point of the story appears when the initial cheese is gobbled up. The mice simply proceed deeper into the maze to search for more cheese. Meanwhile, the humans stay behind to grumble and complain about the unfairness of the situation.

I saw obvious parallels between the book's characters and my work colleagues throughout the years. Some were dragged down by despair that their cheese had been moved. Trends brought change to the status quo that they'd gotten used to. But others remained in cheese discovery mode, prepared to move wherever the cheese was headed.

The cheese metaphor speaks to a critical skill: strategy. Or to be more precise, a strategic plan. Building any strategic plan for a company (and of course yourself) always starts with doing your research and analysis on the relevant inputs that can impact an organization. In this case, that organization is you. To start, we are going to take an external view of what is going on in the world you live in from a work perspective.

That's why we're studying trends. Does the new cheese location align with your personal goals? Can you spot where the cheese will land and position yourself there for better gain? The cheese of work—industry growth projections, organizational structures, career paths, in-demand skills—is moving faster than ever. Figure out where it's going, then plan your moves accordingly. Because some cheese supplies will be suited for your palate. Others will not.

It may help to study what others are doing. Identify patterns beneath their behavior. How are the big companies and noteworthy individuals in your industry (or ones you want to pursue) adapting to the coming changes? What trends are they bracing for or leaning into? What's working for them? What's not?

Ask what the trends mean for your job, your company, your industry, and ultimately, where you want to be. If you spot a trend that means your industry will become automated in two years, do you want to ride out the switch and help manage the new automated industry? Or quickly leap to an adjacent field? Or do something else entirely in a new direction that aligns more closely with your personal goals?

Spotting the Near-Term Opportunities

Some cheese is closer than others. To paraphrase the acclaimed business growth strategist Jay Abraham, get everything you can out of all you've got right now.[38] Where are the cheese crumb trails within sight right now? In other words, what opportunities are available right now to mash up your *existing* skills, interests, jobs, and gigs?

---

38 "Getting Everything You Can Out of What You've Got," Abraham Group, accessed December 31, 2020, www.abraham.com/knowledge_center/getting-every-thing-you-can-out-of-what-youve-got/.

Let's find out. You've probably held several roles by this point in your career. You may have worked at a corporation, in a start-up, as a freelancer, or all three. What skills did you learn from each environment? What about your other interests and hobbies? Most people pack their résumés and social media profiles with hard skills like a new computer programming language. Go beyond. Remember, soft skills are just as important to fluidity. Soft skills may not appear on most résumés, but they're a major reason every hiring process includes face-to-face interviews. We determine hard skills through performance, but we assess soft skills through interaction.

Consider *Dilbert* creator and *New York Times* best-selling author Scott Adams's concept of the "talent stack."[39] Talent stacking is where we take our diverse set of soft and hard skills that we intentionally (or accidentally) learned proficiency in and stack them in a way to augment one another.

For example, a graphic design specialist who runs a YouTube channel on the side can leverage her graphic design knowledge to produce beautiful videos. She can also leverage her video production skills at her graphic design job. Someone with only graphic design or only video production skills is at a distinct disadvantage. Every person has value to offer their employers, clients, customers, users, subscribers, target market, or the general public. You probably have abilities and experiences you have yet to cash in on.

Think about your own talent stack. What value do you have to offer? Are there gaps in that value where additional knowledge, experience, or certification would allow you to earn more? How can you fill those gaps to increase your value and earning potential?

If you spot a market trend in a direction where you lack basic understanding of a crucial skill, you're going to feel frustrated as you watch others snatch up that cheese. When you notice these gaps in your skill set, you can likely find opportunities to fill them. Skill building is essential to fluidity, and we'll return to it in a later chapter. For now, it's

---

39   Scott Adams, "How To Fail at Almost Everything with Scott Adams," YouTube video, www.youtube.com/watch?v=Ac8OOeaIgFo.

important to know that trendspotting involves awareness of the market-able, profitable skills you have now *and* the ones you still need.

Fluidity requires the ability to seamlessly switch from in person to virtual, from cubicle to open office. But trendspotting forces you to get clear on which work environments better suit the way you operate—and how you can transition to them sooner rather than later. Some people do well in a loud, chaotic office with limited alone time, while most get quickly overwhelmed and experience limited productivity. Perhaps you prefer collaborating with dozens of people every day on projects. Many do. Others would rather get to work, check in with one or two people per day, and be done with it.

To identify what your ideal work environment is, ask yourself:

- What have I liked about each of the environments I've worked in?
- What have I disliked?
- Where did I feel most engaged and productive?
- What sort of work excites me right away?

Answering these questions helps you make decisions that bring you into better alignment. For example, you may work well on a fast-paced team but feel stuck and isolated on tedious projects that crawl toward completion. Companies across all industries are shifting toward agile project management with short-term milestones rather than long-term deadlines, so a job or department change would be in perfect alignment with this trend.

Spotting new opportunities that are close to you right now isn't the only goal of self-assessment. Can you better leverage your own skills in your current world? Is there a different role in your current company that would become even more beneficial to the business? Can you better apply your existing skills and experience to your current role or scale up your side hustle without overhauling your routine?

This brings us to one final note about spotting near-term opportunities. The immediate value you can provide companies or customers is more than your work history or a list of services. Value combines the story of your experiences, the skills you've gained, and the unique way you've been able to leverage all of it to produce tangible outcomes. You are your own best asset.

Spotting the Challenges and Threats

Your fluid ability to alter your work arrangements ahead of and along with trends gives you a powerful resilience. You'll need that resilience because challenges will arise faster than ever. Getting blindsided can overwhelm your ability to adapt, leaving you scrambling instead of building value.

Challenges to your personal goals and threats to your income security will arise from several places. Monitor these like your career depends on them. You can do this easily by setting up a simple weekly Google Alert that notifies you about disruptions to your industry, employer, and competitors. This will put you miles ahead of others in the cheese maze.

Another way to do this is follow Jon Krinn's lead. Foodies know Jon as a Washington, DC–based chef extraordinaire. In the throes of the Great Recession, Jon's restaurant was one among thousands that went out of business. Through that demise, Jon realized he needed better business sense if he was ever going to make money from his cuisine passion, knowledge, and skills again. For Jon, that meant getting business experience—and getting paid for it. He had bills to pay and no time for school. Through his old restaurant patrons, Jon had connections with Booz Allen Hamilton, a global management consulting firm where he landed a job in strategic marketing. After working there for five years, he decided to pivot back into the restaurant business while still working remotely at his corporate job. Parallel pathing gave him both the freedom to pursue the new business and manage its risks. For Jon, spotting challenges and threats became natural after learning from failure. Knowing what could go wrong allowed him to plan accordingly. When COVID-19 happened, Jon, unlike many other restaurateurs, was ready, and he found a way to quickly control the uncontrollable. He got out to market quickly by publishing a takeout menu website, diversifying the product offerings, and creating unique customer experiences all while keeping operations running smoothly while competitors were shut down indefinitely. Business is now thriving because Jon learned the hard way what would limit traction—then planned accordingly.

Now, let's talk about you and the challenges and threats facing your career mashup. We're first going to look at each dynamic to research so you can get a holistic view of what's happening. Then you'll be able to do your "homework" to see where your cheese is going to be moved. I suggest you read up on who's hiring, firing, and taking over companies and what companies are being created. You can also collate best practices you've seen in your space and envision potentialities of those trends in your space—sometimes best practices are forced by who has the biggest wallet.

Let's start with industry.

Industry

Whatever affects your industry impacts you personally. Could your industry be made irrelevant due to changes in technology and innovation? What threats do you see on the horizon that may automate, shrink, or complicate your current industry? Are the traditional approaches to servicing customers ripe for disruption? Where are there opportunities to make a more profound impact? Keep yourself up to date on these like you're a CEO. After all, you are the CEO of you.

Another professional whose career mashup we can learn from is Annette Grotheer, MD MPH. She's always had a goal of doing good from an early age and eventually saw health care as a pathway to doing so. In Annette's case, her target audience is actually a segment of patients she saw as underserved, African American men. She is founder of The Shop Docs, a nonprofit that brings health education and screenings to men's barbershops in African American neighborhoods.[40] This focus on The Shop Docs mashes up Annette's medical degrees, her passion for health justice, and her knowledge of both minority health outcome disparities and access to those populations. It gives her clear purpose by delivering preventative care to the minority community. If Annette had only attempted to treat these patients through traditional methods, she would have faced significant structural and perceptual challenges in doing so. Her story offers multiple lessons to us all.

Company (and Competition)

Not all companies are healthy. And every company faces constant change. Is your company stable? Is your CEO knowledgeable and thriving, or struggling to adapt to the new world of work? Is the market thriving, or is your company's share shrinking? Could there be layoffs in the future?

Your company's success may also create threats. Is your company doing so well that a larger company plans to acquire it or merge with it? Will jobs become redundant, including yours? For a good tell for disruption, notice how competitors are faring. Follow their official accounts on social media. Subscribe to their newsletters. Check up on their website's about page every now and then to see who they're hiring. What are industry analysts or other credible trendspotters saying? Are there new regulations, new technology, a world event, or some other change that is weakening competing companies' foothold in your industry? If so, prepare yourself. Sometimes change is an avalanche. Just as often, it's a glacier. Whatever threats overcome your competitors may also reach you sooner than later.

---

40   Richard Westlund, "Miller School Student Named to Forbes '30 Under 30' List for Program Addressing Health Disparities," Invent UM, University of Miami Miller School of Medicine, January 14, 2020, https://physician-news.umiamihealth.org/miller-school-student-named-to-forbes-30-under-30-list-for-work-to-address-health-disparities/.

Job Function

As the business of work changes, so do the individual positions that need to be filled. Whole new jobs are created with each industry shift, while old positions once thought indispensable suddenly disappear. Even if your job functions still exist, they may inevitably change to catch up with new technology and market needs. How will the functional skill sets of your current position change in the future? Will your function be less important or more important?

We have a lot to learn about this from journalist-turned-entrepreneur Stephane Fitch. The former Forbes Chicago bureau chief predicted that digital media would blow up journalism . . . years before it happened. Technology displaces many jobs once considered safe. In Stephane's case, he realized the industry's days were numbered simply because unpaid independent creators were doing his industry's work. He saw a decline in new newspaper subscriptions at the same time he observed a mass switch to social media as the news source. He also noticed that individuals outside journalism who simply had a camera or a smartphone became reporters, creating content that went viral. And Stephane knew that the best journalism happens where the stories are, not where the news companies are. So he built his own content development agency, hired former coworkers to create long-form stories, and now provides a full spectrum of editorial services from corporate communications to writing seminars.

The slow fade of once-secure employment is a concern in full-time salaried jobs, hourly labor, and in freelancing alike. The economy changes by the minute to meet market needs, particularly the gig economy. For example, when businesses of all sizes needed help taking their workforce virtual during COVID-19, freelancers who specialized in digital document management, intranet configuration, and virtual event planning were booked solid. Whether or not they intentionally positioned themselves to add extraordinary value during the big shift from in person to online is irrelevant. What matters is that when challenges called, opportunity answered.

You, too, can capitalize on changes that affect your job. Remember your income portfolio. The more high-value jobs you can get done in one company or within one industry, the better off you'll be. Prepare when it's easy, and you'll be prepared when it's not.

All of this has been building toward the following exercise.

Spotting the Macro Trends

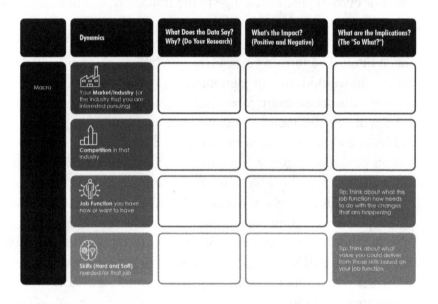

Here are a couple of questions to think about as you do your research.

- What are you seeing as the bigger-picture goals of the company based on what's going on in the market, industry, and competition?
- How will that ultimately impact your job function and the skills that will and won't be needed? Is there any place that you can come in and fill the gap?

In this exercise, it's all about building your analytical skills. It's about gathering relevant information and turning it into insight and implications that could directly impact you.

Spotting the Long-Term Potential

A skilled investor's portfolio includes both short-term risks and measured plays to win the long game. Like an investor, you're working toward something. You want to build the business of you to last.

In personal finance, a common objective is to retire early with enough passive income to cover expenses and with enough principal left over to leave the next generation with an inheritance. So what are you working toward? Challenges and threats will force us to scramble, to try new things at the drop of a hat, and to create our own new income streams. Even so, you can employ long-term strategies to make yourself indispensable to employers, clients, and consumers across industries and across the world.

For example, I know a young freelance writer who acquired three writing degrees over an eight-year period so he could position himself as academically credentialed rather than simply experienced. Higher credentials meant he could charge higher rates. As he's grown his business, he's lived frugally. Unlike the typical freelancer, he has invested profits from his writing business into residential real estate. Last I spoke with him, he was over halfway to covering his living expenses through his rental properties' revenue. That's playing to win.

When searching for opportunities to protect your future financial stability, ask yourself the all-important "so what" questions:

- New technologies are automating jobs in my industry. So what does that mean for my role?
- My company is merging with a larger company. So what does that mean for my position?
- My clients have been asking my advice on other projects outside my expertise. So what skills should I learn to increase my income?

Collecting market data enables you to answer these questions. Shifting patterns you notice today will impact you months or years from now. Try writing down all the changes you can imagine might take place around your current position, in immediately adjacent roles, and in the surrounding industry.

For example, let's say you took a couple of semesters of computer programming at a local community college. You became proficient with JavaScript through free online tutorials and your own fun projects. The education and experience together landed you a day job at a local media agency. All you do every day is program web apps for your employer's clients. Because you're a trendspotter, you've noticed a shift in online freelance marketplace job postings. Alongside JavaScript programming gigs are Python programming jobs, a programming language used for AI. Sooner rather than later, these companies will ask your media agency for help on their machine learning projects. The future is artificially intelligent, and somebody needs to program it. It might as well be you. As a fluid thinker, you find the simplest path toward Python proficiency. Once again, you take a class and watch online tutorials. With a full-time job, you don't have as much free time as you used to, but you know you'll be getting paid to program Python sooner or later. Maybe next you'll pick up Solidity, the new blockchain programming language. It's highly likely that Python and Solidity are not the last languages you'll learn, especially if you're in your twenties, thirties, or even forties.

Assessing, learning, improving, and expanding are nonnegotiables. There is no final destination. Things change too fast. Who knows what innovation has in store for us over the next twenty to fifty years? That's the point of considering your long-term potential. Not even the most attentive, skilled trendspotters know exactly what will happen. That's why you keep tabs on changes in the here and now as well as the bigger, longer picture. Your goal is to match if not exceed the fast pace of the market to find a sweet spot to flow in that meets your personal goals.

Read the trends, engage the opportunities, dodge the threats, and keep going. This is a never-ending process. That shouldn't scare you but excite you. You have unlimited potential to become the most realized version of yourself. Keep assessing at every step. A bias for action is great, but think through the repercussions and outcomes before you act. In plain terms, always look before you leap. And look again after you leap. Always be looking.

Taking Action: Thinking, Assessing, and Evaluating *You*

To leverage yourself properly, you're going to have to be brutally honest with yourself. Where are your strengths? Your weaknesses? It's time to dive more deeply into an internal view of you to determine a potential path of where you want to go.

Inventory Your Skills

Take an absolutely ruthless inventory of all your hard and soft skills. Find a quiet place to sit and make a list, either on paper or in a document. Keep your skills list easily accessible so you can keep adding to it as new skills occur to you. Hard skills, like managing people or web design, are usually the first you'll think of, but soft skills may take additional thought.

Think through all your previous jobs and recreational experiences. Start with your recent work experience, but then dig deeper. If you worked at a fast food restaurant, you know how to run a cash register. If you played high school football, you might have increased upper body strength. If you were in the speech and debate club, you probably have a knack for public speaking. If you performed in your college's Shakespeare plays, you may have above-average memorization skills.

Here are a few more examples of soft skills to get your list started:

- eager for connected teamwork
- effective communication skills
- a solution-focused approach
- responsible about deadlines

These examples focus on mindset, personal qualities, and cultivated discipline. And that's exactly what soft skills are—personal qualities you've built that aren't listed in the employment description at your previous jobs. Remember that you are your own product, marketed to the world. You aren't merely describing yourself in terms of concrete capability, as with hard skills, but as a nuanced individual with a unique array of underlying abilities not listed in your instruction manual.

Assessing yourself as your own product and ruthlessly listing your qualities lets you get to know who you really are. This list helps you understand your wealth of experience and what you really know.

Understand Your Value

Without a deep understanding of what value you bring, you won't be able to leverage yourself as your own best asset. Now that you've listed your skills and best qualities, take a step back and scan for achievements.

What does your story look like from an accomplishments perspective? This doesn't simply mean awards, certificates, and degrees. Look at each company you've worked with and ask:

- What value did I get from each company?
- What value did I offer?
- How can I apply all of this value to future companies?

It's not just the day-to-day tasks that you accomplished. What impact did you have on your team? On the project? On the whole organization? Your value goes well beyond numbers on a sheet.

Your impact may be invisible if your previous company collapsed under an ineffective CEO. What value did you provide even as the company struggled? Where are your previous coworkers now? Where did the employees that you trained go? Did you help cultivate better workers who thrived as they spread out into the world of work?

Then consider:

- How do I learn to generate value at a higher level?
- Based on the value I generate now, where can I fill market gaps created by trends I see?
- Where can I become the best solution to others' problems?

Look at your whole life experience so you understand the consequences of each move you've made in the past. You've got a unique set of experience and skills—use that to your advantage!

We're now ready to conduct your own self-assessment of what works and what doesn't. To determine a potential path for where you want your career to go, you also have to get grounded in what works for you.

It's important to get external perspectives about what makes you, you. This can illuminate strengths, skills, and areas of opportunity that you wouldn't have even considered from those who know you best.

This is called a 360-degree review in many companies. It's where bosses, peers, and subordinates give feedback into your performance—what you do well, what you can improve upon, and where you have potential.

Another way of looking at this is a Voice of the Customer exercise. In business, it's common for companies to get customer feedback and insights from those they have done business with. This provides another lens that can provide unbiased input on what truly makes a company unique, why they are better than their competitors, and what they could improve upon.

Now it's your turn to do this as your own company.

Select up to five people who know your work style, work product, personality, and interests across various facets of your life. I recommend the following people: former bosses, coworkers, close friends or family members, former/current employees (if relevant), and even former vendors you've worked with. Ideally pick one from each group. You want a variety of perspectives, as they will all have a different take on you based on where they sit.

Now schedule one-on-one interviews with them. Ask for a half hour of their time at a minimum, but if you can get more, great. Here are some questions to get you started:

- What qualities do you think best describe me and my work style?
- Where do you feel I add the most value to an organization and to others? (e.g., process, deliverable, communication style, etc.)

- What do you feel makes me unique? What is my secret sauce and why?
- What specific skills do you feel best represent my abilities? (Ask for both hard and soft skills.)
- What work environments do you think would leverage my talents best? Why?
- What do you feel is a strength of mine that I am not leveraging to its fullest?
- What is a developmental area that you feel is one that I need to work more on? Why?
- Is there a specific industry, field, or role that you think I should explore? Why?
- Where do you feel I might have struggled in the past in terms of being able to leverage my full potential? Why?
- Where have you seen me feel the most fulfilled in my career?

I suggest you record the interview so you don't struggle to remember all that valuable data later. You can use Zoom or QuickTime on your computer or use the voice memo feature on your phone. Then transcribe the conversation using online tools like Descript or Temi, which are free to start. Or, if you want to use a paid version so you get 100 percent accuracy, you can go with services like Rev.com or GoTranscript.com.

Once you've collected all the input, analyze the information. Look for themes and patterns based on the responses you get. Understand why they said what they did and align it to what you've identified as environments, roles, and experiences that align best with your interests, strengths, and skills.

Take a look at your summary of implications from the macro analysis exercise and compare it to what you've learned about yourself, the micro.

- Where do you see alignment to what you could do in the near term and where you could go in the long term?
- Where can your skills/experience/interests align to the trends that could be happening in your space? Are there opportunities where you can come in and be the solution?

- Do your interests align to ways that you can fill in those white spaces? How can you start to integrate your personal interests to help your current business or even start your own?
  - Could you generate value at a higher and different level?
  - What will it take for you to build those skills to be that solution?

As you look to the future, you can probably already see yourself generating value at higher and different levels. Based on how you could generate value, how does that fit with those gaps you identified based on the trends you saw? Where could you come and be the solution? These questions may take weeks if not months (or longer) to answer, and that's OK. Later in the book, we'll outline a plan for you to acquire the knowledge and build the skills you need to be that solution.

Mastering the ability to assess the opportunities and threats that the coming trends will create is itself an essential skill. By learning to identify trends, challenges, and opportunities in advance, you're able to take action today and in the future. You're filling gaps and gaining advantage over the people who can't or won't study the trends.

CHAPTER 4

Creating
Your Compass

Remember those shopping mall guide signs? The ones with the little "you are here" dot on the map? Let's bring those back to orient ourselves on our career mashup journey. By now, you've learned how to spot market trends, both long-term shifts to prepare for and near-term trends you can leverage. You also understand why it's important to stay on top of new information—we can't seize opportunities we don't know exist.

Now, what are you supposed to do with all that data? Enter the strategic plan. Because information itself doesn't help you unless it drives action. If you have no plan, you're executing aimlessly. This chapter's goal is to make your newfound awareness work for you. Together, we'll plan your career mashup steps in advance, so you can pivot and remain aligned with both passion and potential.

The art and science of strategic planning are familiar to anyone who's attended business school or simply took a business class. Starting and running a business without a plan is like applying for a job without a résumé. Mountain hiking without shoes. Sailing without a rudder or paddles. Oh, they're all possible. But the downsides are painfully obvious.

In business, in a career, in any endeavor in life, you can't advance toward your goal if you don't know where your goal is in the first place. You can't succeed in the business of work if you don't have a plan. And without a plan, you can't communicate to your team what your desired direction is so they can help you. Because if you're just executing all over the place, people can't get on the bus to support you in realizing the vision of where you want to be. Your plan is your lifeline in chaos and your road map while traveling.

Centuries ago, explorers, navigators, and pioneers needed to know what direction they were traveling as they ventured into the unknown. They trusted their compass to tell them where they were in relation to their surroundings so they could better plan their journey toward the ultimate destination.

With this chapter, you're creating your very own career compass: a directional guide rather than a linear one with turn-by-turn instructions; a method for orienting yourself back to your main path, no matter how many side roads you have to take along the way.

Why a Compass?

By far, the most common career struggle I see that spans all living generations is uncertainty. *What should I do next?* Opportunities yank us to and fro. No two career mashups are alike. Our heads spin with indecision because we're in uncharted territory. This job or that job? This client or that? This skills training or another? All of everything, all of the things, and all of the above? So many decisions.

That's why we need a true compass. A means of finding our way, our "north." Lost in the wilderness of work, we need a directional guide to keep us proceeding toward our desired destination. Simply put, the strategic plan is that compass. It provides the much-needed clarity when you're deciding what to do, what not to do, what to start doing, and what to stop.

And don't worry if your plan isn't perfect. Perfection isn't the goal. Neither is rigidity. Fluidity is the state of things, the new normal. Revising your plan is as simple as consulting a real compass. *Looks like we're off the path here. Better adjust course. Done.* So we don't get too far ahead of ourselves into the unknown, we're going to start small. Test. Learn. Proceed. Your strategic plan can and should change as you grow. Because your goals fluidly change. Because you yourself will be changing, becoming better informed, better skilled, and better paid. Yes, we'll be writing your plan—creating your compass—but treat it like a living document. It is one. Because you'll be updating it for the rest of your life.

Turning "So What?" into "Now What?"

When studying market trends, you know to ask the fundamental "so what" questions. For example:

- The market is trending toward automation of my current position. **So what** does that mean for my future?
- A leading CEO in my field is opening up a new company. **So what** does that mean for the industry and for me personally?

Understanding how a trend will impact you is crucial. More important is taking action with that information. Turning the "so what" into the "now what" looks like:

- The market is trending toward automation of my current position. My job may be dissolved. **Now what** can I do to shift into an advantageous position and leverage my skill sets? Perhaps as a consultant to help design better automation technologies?
- A thought leader is leaving an established company to found a start-up. They're likely going to open a new market. **Now what** do I want to do? Stay with my company and adjust to the

market splash or try to get in with that new company and grow with them?

Turning "so what" into "now what" gets you thinking about what you *want* to do next. If you're feeling stuck on what you want, don't worry. You're about to learn how to articulate your wants into a constant guide that will never leave you feeling unsure of yourself ever again.

Where Do You Want to Be?

You've studied the trends in your industry, so you see where things are headed. You've taken a thoughtful look at your own priorities and passions. You know what you like and dislike. You know where your natural talents lie, and you understand your skill sets. So where do you want to go next?

Strategic planning is about defining your direction (or potential directions) based on connecting the dots between the trends and your interests and goals, and then outlining how you are going to make it happen. Sounds simple enough. But what about when you're pulled between conflicting ideas? You have all these aspirations. That's great. How are you going to "parallel path" them into reality? In our fluid new world, compensation is not the deciding factor. *Which job, gig, client, customer, or opportunity should I take? The one that pays more, of course!* Yeah . . . no. Business isn't the only metric. If none of your goals are personal, you're missing half the picture.

When social entrepreneur Meghan French Dunbar joined me on *Strategic Momentum*, she repeated the necessity of personal passions in a career plan. Because that was her job. As cofounder and former CEO of Conscious Company Media, Meghan helped people remain purpose driven over the course of their careers. To her, strategic planning done right is about aligning who you are, what you do, who you serve, and why. And that focus on you is so fundamental. When your work has a positive impact, it feels good. You're getting paid and giving back without losing what's important to you. That's sustainable.

And yes, that may mean your ideal work involves multiple part-time opportunities that don't add up to an eight-to-five you're qualified for. That's perfectly fine. In fact, it's the right decision to choose work that allows you more free time with your significant other over a position that pays twice as well with one or two evenings free a week. If that's what you want, of course. If your priority is your family, asking yourself what you want and clarifying your personal priorities alongside your achievement goals means you're more aligned with the nontraditional work roles or situations. Because you'll experience true fulfillment. That's your compass at work.

What's the Gap?

When you map out your career trajectory and identify what you want, the next step is to see what's missing. What gaps exist between your current skill set and where you want to be? What other gaps do you need to fill before you can cross the bridge to your future, and how do you systematically overcome these obstacles? Do you need to change industries? Is this a huge jump into an adjacent field or even something you've never tried before? If your industry is losing to automation, or if a whole new industry provides a golden opportunity, you may take a flying leap into a whole new field. This can be a fantastic way of building entirely new skill sets that complement your existing skills.

Do you need to change companies? Sometimes where you're at is just not a good fit. The old, prerecession, prepandemic business world saw many people sit in one company for their entire lives and stay loyal to a brand. In the new fluid world, people shift in and out of companies according to their personal and professional needs. It could be that your current CEO is running your company to the bottom of the industry. Or maybe you've just bumped the cap on what you can achieve in your current organization. Maybe you want to start your own company and become your own CEO. Don't get bogged down by the idea that you must stay within your current company.

Do you need to change roles? Maybe the company isn't the problem, but you just haven't found your place within it. If you've been working as a data analyst for your team and you've realized you can't stand doing it anymore, but you've always longed to interact with customers directly, maybe it's time to think about shifting into PR, sales, marketing, or customer relations.

Do you need to change your work environment? Maybe it's just the office, the floor, or the layout of the place. Are you tired of the same four walls? Do you feel pulled toward a bigger city and can transfer to another branch of the same company? Are you sick of the commute and need to apply to work remotely? What sort of work environment is most conducive to your success and your future plans?

Do you need to change your manager? Or coworkers? Is the office buzzing with negative energy? Sometimes you're stuck with a boss who just doesn't appreciate you as an individual. And some teams are so toxic that work becomes nearly impossible. It could be that you need to get away from your current team and into a new group of people more aligned with your own values and principles. And even if you're not fleeing a bad circumstance, it's always possible there's a better fit out there that will help cultivate you into the person you want to become.

Do you need to change your skills, both hard and soft? Really, the answer is *always yes.* So ask yourself, "What changes to my skills need to happen soon? What near-term changes and long-term changes need to happen to deepen my skill sets in the right ways? What priority skills should I be studying tonight? What skill am I mastering this month?"

Building a Strategic Plan

Kevin Garton spoke on my *Strategic Momentum* podcast about strategic planning. Kevin is the head of marketing communications North America at Epson today, but he reached the executive level on a winding road through Fortune 500, scale-ups and start-ups in a myriad of industries: financial services, consumer products, enterprise software, and internet media. He's drafted and rewritten hundreds of strategic plans, which, again, is basically what you're doing for your career.

The most important aspect of any strategy, Kevin told me, is to make choices that enable you to keep a competitive edge in your market niche. The second aspect is implementation. So many companies (and the people who work there) make plans but never implement them. Kind of like a personal bucket list of "maybe someday" dreams.

If you want a successful plan, plan to follow it. The best method I've found for writing implementable strategic plans is the **GhOST** method.

- Goal
- Objective
- Strategies
- Tactics

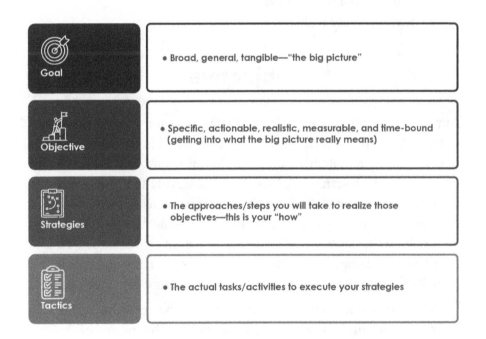

Goal
- Broad, general, tangible—"the big picture"

Objective
- Specific, actionable, realistic, measurable, and time-bound (getting into what the big picture really means)

Strategies
- The approaches/steps you will take to realize those objectives—this is your "how"

Tactics
- The actual tasks/activities to execute your strategies

Let's look at each step in depth now.

Goal

Keep it broad, general, and tangible. This is "the big picture" of what you hope to accomplish. It's a descriptive statement of what you aim to achieve, personally and/or professionally. And this is a singular goal, one solid change you plan to make. It is more qualitative than quantitative in nature. When you write the description, focus on what outcomes you want to create when you're done. It's envisioning that end state. Here are a few examples.

- Find and keep a healthy work-life balance.
- Align the work I do with my passions and interests.
- Pivot into a new role at work.
- Move into a new industry.
- Switch career paths.

Objective

Aim for a specific, actionable, realistic, measurable, and time-bound statement. Think of this as the next level of detail in realizing your goal. If your goal is a statement of what the ideal outcome will look like, the objective is description of the act of achieving that. Be concise and thorough about your statement with a definite measurement of success.

Here is where we get a bit more realistic and measurable. Your objectives outline the necessary steps to achieve each primary goal. Think of objectives as actions you'll take. That means the language will include directives like "pivot," "increase," or "build." Here are some examples.

- Switch to a flexible work schedule by the end of this year.
- Launch my business and earn five clients by the end of this year.
- Move from an associate to a manager in nine months.
- Earn 10 percent more at the end of six months.

Strategies

Mark down the approaches and steps you will take to realize your objectives. This is where you write the "how" of your plan. This continues to add more fidelity to the actions that will get you to success. List as many as necessary. Some examples include the following.

- Develop my personal brand.
- Position myself as a thought leader with content.
- Grow my network with business leaders outside my industry.
- Develop my hard and soft skills for the job I want.

Tactics

These are the actual tasks and activities to execute your strategies. You're going to ask yourself what skills and opportunities you can leverage for maximum success. These are also time bound and can easily be measured. As an example, you may list a number of specific industry conferences you'll attend to network and gain new insights. Or the research you've been doing all along may fit perfectly into your new goals. In fact, that's the point of market research. Check out these examples:

- Set up one to three coffee meetings each week with people in my network.
- Sign up for online courses to learn new skills.
- Work with a mentor/coach to uplevel my soft skills.
- Create a personal website/portfolio and start blogging.

Once you've gotten your GhOST written, simply place everything in a spreadsheet like in the example below.

Sample Strategic Plan

FastBook Advisors founder Dan Yu advocates strongly for identifying your goals. As a strategic business advisor and talent agent, Dan helps connect people and companies, and he knows how important a plan is to both hiring and being hired.

One of the biggest obstacles to successful candidate and job position pairing, says Dan, is that many job hunters aren't clear on what they want. They can't articulate specific career goals or what they want their next step to be. Their profile on LinkedIn is minimal or it contains a mess of information without any specific target for all their ambition. They're desperate to run but don't have a direction.

They don't have a compass. This lack of direction leads job hunters to constantly and blindly apply for new jobs, with their applications inevitably going into a black hole.

So you can have clarity on your strategic career plan, here's an example of a finished one.

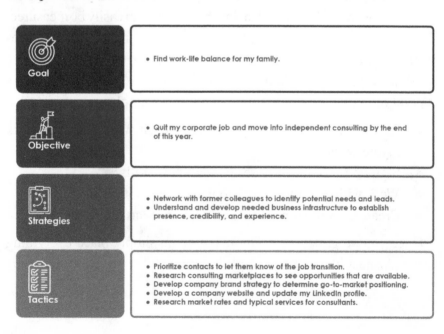

Goal
- Find work-life balance for my family.

Objective
- Quit my corporate job and move into independent consulting by the end of this year.

Strategies
- Network with former colleagues to identify potential needs and leads.
- Understand and develop needed business infrastructure to establish presence, credibility, and experience.

Tactics
- Prioritize contacts to let them know of the job transition.
- Research consulting marketplaces to see opportunities that are available.
- Develop company brand strategy to determine go-to-market positioning.
- Develop a company website and update my LinkedIn profile.
- Research market rates and typical services for consultants.

Something unusual may occur to you: networking fits in both strategies *and* tactics! Networking is a key ingredient to success and may take place as both a strategy and an asset to leverage. There is really no getting around the importance of networking. Not even for introverts. Podcast superstar Jordan Harbinger has run a top-fifty podcast for over twelve years and has been dubbed "The Larry King of Podcasts." In true fluid fashion, he's also considered a leading expert on social dynamics. Jordan recognizes some people have a hard time feeling motivated to get out and socialize in order to build their networks.

Jordan dishes out some harsh truth for anyone who doesn't network. You're not immune to the consequences of *not* putting yourself out there, he says. You're just being willfully ignorant of the secret game that's being played around you. And you're screwed if you're on the bad end of that. You never know when a relationship could become crucial, so you've got to always be networking to make sure you "dig the well before you're thirsty."

It's a fair bet that networking will belong in both the strategies and tactics sessions for most of your plans. Networking is so critical to your career success, we're devoting an entire chapter to it later in the book.

Measuring Your Success and Setting a Time Frame

What good is a strategic plan without the ability to measure whether or not it's working? You can identify what you want to do, but without a time frame in which to get it done, you'll likely procrastinate and not make the necessary progress you want.

Once you've got your plan, you can add an additional column to keep track of milestones. Using the sample plan, start with putting **timing and success metrics** against your **tactics**. Remember, this is all about taking small steps to help get comfortable with this process. So it might simply look like the number of conferences I'll attend, designate people I need to spend more time with every week, or log in the number of hours doing market research each week. Adding in a success matrix to your plan can look like this:

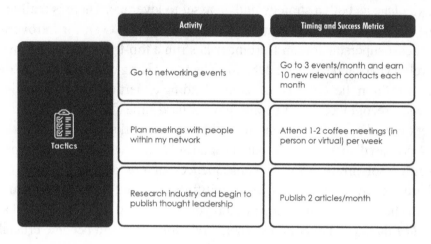

	Activity	Timing and Success Metrics
Tactics	Go to networking events	Go to 3 events/month and earn 10 new relevant contacts each month
	Plan meetings with people within my network	Attend 1-2 coffee meetings (in person or virtual) per week
	Research industry and begin to publish thought leadership	Publish 2 articles/month

Creating Your Compass: Exercise

Formulating where you want to go requires you to have a strategy and plan of action for how to get there. You've studied your market trends and assessed your own skills. Now it's time to map those implications, opportunities, and interests into potential pathways.

Getting It Down on Paper

Start by putting down all of your thoughts on what you want to do and how you think you can get there based on the analysis that you did in Chapter 3. Don't worry about organizing them yet. Just put everything down.

These can be aspirational or specific. Whatever comes to mind. The goal is to just do a brain dump and get them written down.

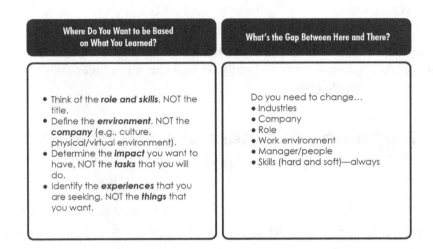

Where Do You Want to be Based on What You Learned?

- Think of the *role and skills*, NOT the title.
- Define the *environment*, NOT the *company* (e.g., culture, physical/virtual environment).
- Determine the *impact* you want to have, NOT the *tasks* that you will do.
- Identify the *experiences* that you are seeking, NOT the *things* that you want.

What's the Gap Between Here and There?

Do you need to change...
- Industries
- Company
- Role
- Work environment
- Manager/people
- Skills (hard and soft)—always

Organizing Your Thoughts

Now group your scattered thoughts. Identify goals and objectives and put them in one list. Tactics go in another list.

If you notice that your goals and objectives list is a lot smaller than your tactics list, don't worry. That's a good thing. You're actually more focused than you might think, and it means you've got solid leverage to help you reach your goals.

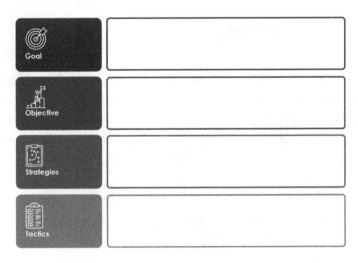

Goal

Objective

Strategies

Tactics

Next, focus on grouping the goals and objectives into similar themes that you might see and bucket them together. Prioritize these groups and identify your top goal or theme. That might be getting a new job or spending more time with family. If you can align objectives to that, great; if not, that's OK.

Mapping the Where and the How (But Let's Start Small)

Now that you've got your goals and objectives sorted by theme, it's time to look at tactics. Align the tactics that you grouped together earlier to what you've identified as your *highest-priority goal* and *corresponding objectives*.

We're thinking big in this exercise, but we are starting small by picking one goal—the most important goal. The intent is to build your confidence in developing your discipline by starting small and not boiling the ocean.

Next, you'll want to list your primary goal and corresponding objectives on the left and your tactics on the right. Draw a line to which tactics would be relevant to bring that goal and objective to life.

Filling in the Holes

Now start to think about where you have gaps in being able to fulfill your goal. Here is where you should start to think about the strategies needed to fulfill your goals and objectives, which may have been a challenge earlier. Before, you had no scaffolding for building your own unique career. Now you do. And now you know where it should go.

That also means there are gaps in your plan. You will realize where these gaps are once you put back into the template your goals, objectives, and tactics, which now should have a hierarchy to them. The strategies area, however, will be empty.

Back to the holes. Are there tactics you haven't identified that are necessary to meet your goals, such as important skills you should develop or hone? What about people you should talk to or resources you need to read up on to better understand the market and industry you want to work in? How would you go about doing that?

You've identified the big picture of what you want. Have you considered all the ways to get there? Conversely, you have all these activities you've been thinking about doing. Do they logically ladder up into what your focused vision of the future against this one goal could look like?

Fill those gaps with additional tactics that will be necessary for you to find success and fulfillment or to refine your goals and objectives to clarify what you really want.

Once you have those in place, start to determine the specific strategies you would need to take based on the unused tactics you've identified.

Next, align timing and success metrics to this initial plan so you can chart your progress. As an example, if you're building a side company, you may target a specific number of followers on your company's social media profile to measure networking. Or you may follow profile analytics and track engagements with a specific number in mind that indicates you've reached the next threshold of community awareness of your brand.

Don't stop here. Continue to do this exercise for all the other goals and objectives you have outlined. You may have multiple strategic plans that you want to pursue to reach both personal and professional goals.

Keep in mind that the tactics you've identified might include proxies for skills that you need to hone or develop. Keep track of those missing skills for later when we discuss how to cultivate your skill sets. Plus, the tactics you have identified for one particular goal might well be the same for others that you have set for yourself.

My point is to go tiny. You've identified your most important goal, and I don't want to deter you here. It's about identifying all the tactics and breaking them down into smaller parts so you feel comfortable actually doing something and creating progress.

Remember to focus on diversifying potential revenue streams, and that comes from creating optionality via parallel pathing. In other words, don't put all your eggs in one basket. Make sure at least one part of your plan involves growing revenue in new directions or finding additional sources to keep your finances growing.

And be realistic about your goals. If one goal is more of a wish—a dream for some far-distant future where you've got unlimited resources—don't prioritize that one just yet. Determine where you're going to get traction and double down on that goal first. Your entire outlook could change with the successful completion of one goal that unlocks multiple new doors.

If you find yourself stuck at any point, draw clarity from the following questions:

- What goals do I have in my personal and professional lives?
- How can I learn to generate value at a higher and different level?
- How do value opportunities fit with gaps I've identified based on the trends I saw?
- Where could I be the solution?
- What will it take for me to build the skills to be that solution?

Sounds labor intensive? It is. And it should be. This isn't busywork or a bucket list; it's your future.

I estimate that your comprehensive, implementable strategic plan could take up to a few hours or even a couple of weeks to fully map out. If that seems like a lot of work for a measly set of charts, ask yourself this: Should I spend two hours mapping out my plan so I know in advance every move I need to make, or would I rather be frustrated and stuck without any idea how to improve?

Remember: 50 percent of your day is doing your job. But 50 percent should be spent working on your career. This is an adage from Dan Yu (thanks, Dan!).

You've Got Your Compass. Now What?

Now that you know in what direction you want to travel, you will never get lost again. Changes may come, and they likely will, but you can rest assured you're prepared if and when they do.

Having a compass means all that paralysis and frustration you felt is a thing of the past. Where others flounder in confusion, you can pick yourself right back up and get to work on the new problems.

Remember to continuously update and rewrite your plans. These aren't set in stone but are living documents that are meant to be changed and revised. When you learn about something that conflicts with an upcoming plan, modify or alter your compass to course correct and spring into action to achieve maximum success!

Your plans are your lifelines in troubled waters, but they also double or triple your running speed even on stable ground. When you know where you want to go and how to get there, nothing can hold you back.

Building your plan gets you ready for what comes next, whatever that may be. If your industry collapses, but your plans are solid, you can rewrite the obsolete points and pivot right to your next goal. You won't get stuck in uncertainty or confusion as everything around you changes.

Change can be frightening. And building plans feels like you're going to cause change to happen. But you're not. Change will happen no matter what. By building a plan, you aren't tempting fate to begin change. Having a plan means you're prepared for the change that must inevitably come. You're hedging your bets against the future and making sure that no matter how the earth shakes, you'll land on at least one solid foot.

Get ready for the change that's coming by building comprehensive and living plans.

CHAPTER 5

Preparing for Change

Y ou've analyzed the trends. You've developed your compass by outlining the objectives, strategies, and tactics to hit your goals. Now you're making your own trail through the new world of work. As your competition falls behind, you gain momentum. You spot an opportunity just ahead of you, and then . . .

You stop. You feel frozen. What now? You can't think or analyze. There are too many factors. Too many risks.

You feel excited, but also anxious. You're unsure how to push forward. You start picturing the worst possible outcomes.

What if I fail?

What if I fail so badly I have to move back in with my parents?

What if I deplete my savings pursuing my passion?

What if everyone who said to pick one career lane and stay there was right?

In the last chapter, we discussed how to build your compass and follow it to achieve your goals. You know how to identify trends, spot opportunities, and align them to your personal desires. You even know how to stay ahead of the competition.

But facts and skills don't stop the fear. Knowing is not the same as feeling. And perceived danger threatens even the smartest CEO.

In fact, one of the greatest threats to your success is your own fear. That fear creates anxiety, procrastination, and ultimately avoidance in moving forward and being in the driver's seat of your future versus being controlled by what others or society deems as the norm. Worry about failure stops us from taking the bold steps needed to seize each opportunity to the fullest.

So how do you fight this fear of the unknown? How do you push through the panic, plunge into the world of what ifs, and pull out your victory?

In order to be successful, we must get to the root cause of what's driving our fear. When you understand fear, you're able to push past it. The more you get past it, the more confidence you build to move in the direction you want. It's all about creating that flywheel effect.

To truly understand and conquer our fear, we must take the time to prepare.

Preparation Is Mental, Not Just Operational

People often attempt to prepare for change and thus manage their fear by focusing on mapping out everything they should or will do. "If I do these steps, I'll have no reason to be afraid." But this doesn't fundamentally address what could hold a person back in the first place.

Preparing to fight fear means first getting to the root of why. That may initially manifest in your emotions. In fact, your actions are not always logical but in fact stem from emotional triggers like fear. If you understand that your fear may be irrational, you can approach it differently. And once you uncover the root cause of that irrationality, you can be rational in your next actions.

It's important to dive headfirst into doing this critical self-analysis instead of shying away from it. You might think it's a waste of time, or maybe you fear what you'll find if you dig deep down. Since you've come this far in the book, I know that's not you. So in this chapter, I'm going to teach you how to understand, face, and manage your fear and even all the other negative emotions that are closely related to it.

Let's look at the fear drawn from being judged by others. What you're doing with your career is most likely counter to the norms and standards that everyone is comfortable with or aware of. Your family may even be in a frenzy about how you're ruining your life by deviating from the traditional path. Your parents may take you aside and ask if your entrepreneurial endeavor has failed yet. They may mean well, but these outside pressures add to your fear—because much of our fear is really about shame. We experience shame (or even guilt) that . . .

- we're doing something different from our family's expectations.
- others don't believe in our vision.
- others disapprove of our choices.

Shame is powerful. As human beings, we have a need to belong, to get approval, and to feel secure. We're terrified of disappointing the ones we love. So we collapse into our fears. Fear of failure. Rejection. Loneliness. Instability.

By now, you have been working toward many of the skills you need to succeed. You're reading this book, which means you already have the necessary drive and ambition. Over the last few chapters you've learned how to start cultivating the proper mindset to thrive in the world of work. Now it's time to recognize that your fear is what can get you stuck. Surprisingly, this is the obstacle most fail to overcome.

But you're going to stay unstuck. Permanently. You're going to lay out a system that breaks down your current fears, and you're going to use it every time you feel afraid from now on. You'll learn to power through your fears and reach the success that's waiting for you on the other side.

You're going to, to quote Susan Jeffers, "Feel the fear and do it anyway." You do this by:

- transforming your fear into excitement
- building your self-confidence

- increasing the positive aspects of what you will be doing
- creating an energy of empowerment

But . . . how? You might be clutching this book, saying, "Connie, this seems so complicated! If powering through fear was that simple, everyone would be doing it!"

It's only simple if you know what you're doing. That's why we'll take it step by step. First, let's look at what common issues can inhibit you from doing the doing rather than thinking of the doing in the first place.

The Common Career Blockers (Emotional versus Rational)

As complicated as each individual may be, many of us fall into the same mental pitfalls. Fear can cause you to act in less strategic ways. It can derail you from the path you need to be on to reach your goal. That's why it's so important to tackle these conscious or even unconscious fears, especially the biggest and most paralyzing.

Here are the most common fears we each may grapple with.

"How Do I Know if I'm Confident Enough?"

If you find yourself worrying about worrying, or trying to obsessively measure your own confidence levels, stop and take a breath. The point is not to have zero fear. The goal is to keep fear from holding you back. Removing certain fears is a means to an end, not the goal itself.

Are you progressing toward your personal and business goals, or are you shying away from risks due to irrational fear? Confidence comes from achievement. Your confidence will grow as you move closer to your goals. You'll find your fears diminishing automatically, and even disappearing around areas where you've achieved success.

Dana Cavalea is the former strength and conditioning coach for the New York Yankees. Building confidence and skill is his entire focus.

He directs clients to start small and build their habits, to go back to the foundation of their lives and cultivate even their automatic routine and response. This builds habitual excellence, which in turn develops confidence.

In other words, start small and don't worry about your confidence level. It will grow with you as you see changes happening.

"But I Haven't Done It Before, and No One Thinks I Can Do It Now."

Imposter syndrome can strike hard. You get a few achievements under your belt, but a bigger challenge comes along. Suddenly you doubt your ability. You worry you're going to fail even though you've succeeded at everything else so far. "Maybe it was all a fluke, and this is where I fall apart!"

This comes from feeling out of your depth and from not trusting yourself. The explicit expectations of others are a whole other issue. Our family and friends can be the best and worst supporters. Any parent can understand this paradox as we watch our children take those first precious steps and promptly fall straight to the floor, bumping their chin, and screaming like the world is ending. Our family wants us to succeed, but they're also terrified we'll fall flat on our faces.

Let me remind you that you aren't doing this for the approval of others. You're out to achieve success on your own terms for your own satisfaction. Those who love you will celebrate your accomplishments regardless of whether they understand your business choices.

Aim for success first and let your family breathe a sigh of relief when you've made it a few steps without falling down. The same advice holds true for dealing with imposter syndrome. You're not doing any of this for accolades or approval. Overall success is your real goal. You're going to face setbacks sometimes. That doesn't mean you're a fraud. It means you're learning. Worry less about what others will think of you if you make a mistake. Focus instead on learning from each mistake and improving your performance the next time.

Don't let your audience impact your performance. They aren't the ones with skin in the game. You are.

"I'm Worried about Being Judged."

Many worry what others outside of their family will think of them. Not just their friends and coworkers—they worry what will be said or written about them by anyone watching their rise (and their anticipated fall).

What's the best way to stop worrying about what others will say? Remember that the people who matter will be rooting for you. And the people with enough free time to make snide comments about your choices don't matter. They can't get their head around the concept of doing things differently because they are unlikely to want to make drastic changes themselves. Some people just don't address their own fear problems, and they work to validate their choices by putting others down.

The reality is that it takes courage to do something different, to shift from the known to the unknown. In fact, many are envious that you are being contrarian and taking the road that has been less traveled but has greater potential. It's jealousy and envy that they are feeling.

Stop working so hard to impress people who don't want you to succeed. Focus on succeeding the way *you* want to and let others say what they want.

"Why Do I Always Feel So Much Pressure?"

The dual pressure to please others and succeed for ourselves can be a good thing. But taken to the extreme, the compulsion to succeed becomes detrimental to you mentally and physically. This is often born of insecurity, a need for approval, and a craving to be liked.

If you feel the pressure to succeed at every turn without even a single step backward, this will destroy your chances of happiness and long-term success. It is impossible to never make a misstep, and adapting to your mistakes is vital to correcting your pathway. A compass is useful but not infallible, and you will take occasional detours. If you let the slightest imperfection destroy you, you'll never truly succeed.

Give yourself permission to make mistakes and break the mold. Embrace the lessons you learn from them and come back stronger, smarter, and ready to thrive.

"If I Fail, I've Failed Everyone Else I Care About."

Fear of failure that will bring shame upon others is very real. No one wants to make their parents look bad. This extends beyond family to mentors, coaches, guides, and bosses. If your mentor sticks her neck out for you and you bomb your project, what will people think of her? What will she, in turn, think of you?

The people who genuinely care about you aren't in this to look good. They want you to succeed. They recognize that's going to take some trial and error. If you aren't sure what they expect, it may help to have an honest conversation.

"How will you feel if I don't succeed every time? Will you still love me/care about me/work with me?"

They of course will say yes. They may even laugh at your fear. And hearing their reassurance may finally put to bed this fear of your inevitable imperfections.

The Battle We All Fight: Catastrophizing Failure

Let me introduce you to a word you need to memorize: **catastrophizing**.

> Catastrophizing (noun): irrational thinking that something is far worse than it actually is.

Catastrophizing can generally take two different forms: making a catastrophe out of a current situation and making a catastrophe out of a future situation.

When you picture one small mistake leading to a domino effect that ends with you bankrupt, that's catastrophizing.

When you imagine that putting out your perspectives on social issues will result in others thinking you have no credibility and you're a fraud, that's catastrophizing.

When deciding on the carpet color for your office paralyzes you with fear that the wrong color will upset guests, that's catastrophizing.

These are extreme examples. But that's the point: catastrophizing takes normal concerns and cranks them into overdrive until you're frantic.

If fear gets you stuck, catastrophizing can plant your feet in quicksand. All your worst insecurities convince you that everything is a life-or-death battle. You project that negative thinking, and you start to believe that's what will happen. Your mind shifts from positive outcomes to hedging against this fear of failure.

I want you to imagine working for a boss like that. Would you stick around for more than a day? Most likely not. Now, how do you think you and your coworkers will feel if you catastrophize? Imagine mentoring someone like that. How exhausting. You'd be dealing with a panic attack at every decision point. You won't hold on to valuable mentors if you catastrophize.

So what's the magic bullet to kill catastrophic thinking?

Reality.

Here are a few reality checks:

Reality Check 1: You're Still Here

Right now, right here, you're still alive. Not only living, but poised to transform yourself into a relentless force in the new world of work. This is a major accomplishment.

Remember award-winning chef Jon Krinn? COVID-19 devastated the restaurant industry. But Jon thrived. That's because he learned from his experience during the 2008 recession and was prepared for change this time around. Now he's come through the worst all the stronger for it.

Jon found the courage to act boldly during the COVID-19 shutdown. His restaurant is thriving due to his skill sets and confidence. Fear doesn't stop him from getting what he wants because he remembers the obstacles he's already conquered.

You have also refused to give up when so many others have caved in. Give yourself that due credit.

Reality Check 2: Failure Is an Accomplishment

Because the *second* part of failure . . . is success.

The goal is not to never fail but to learn from each failure. It's through trial and error that we grow. When you fail, you learn an important new rule: that method didn't work. Then you try something new. Rick Lindquist, founder of LegUp Health and former CEO of Zane Benefits, spoke about failure and shared his motto: "Fail fast, fail often." How can a CEO thrive with a mindset like that?

"Fail fast, fail often" means you maintain a bias toward action—even if that action ends up being wrong. It's better to try, fail, and learn something than to stay locked in place and unable to act. Staying frozen lets someone else grab your chance and leaves you with hollow regret.

Would you rather try, fail, and learn before you succeed? Or avoid looking foolish and never accomplish anything? Learning from failure means you're always on the path to growth and success.

Reality Check 3: Whatever Doesn't Kill Us Makes Us More Successful

As you grow through trial and error, your ability to manage the twists and turns of the unexpected strengthens. Small mistakes and failures won't wound you as deeply as they once did because you've proven you can survive them. Your confidence *will* build because the positives will outweigh the negatives.

Catastrophe is less of a threat because you've already weathered the worst and come back twice as strong.

Reality Check 4: If You Win It's Because You've Learned

If you win, you can repeat your success by using the methods you've perfected. If you lose, you've still learned something. There is no real loss. "Losing" only happens when you stop trying. As John C. Maxwell says, "Sometimes you win. Sometimes you learn."

You've learned. You're smarter, stronger, and better equipped to rise. Even if the worst does happen, you're prepared to weather it and succeed anew.

The Psychology of Change

Take a good look at the following framework.

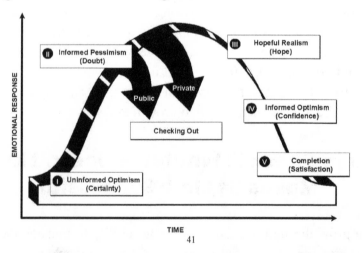

41

---

41   Daryl Conner, "Change Is Easy When People Like It, Right?" Conner Partners, April 24, 2012, www.connerpartners.com/frameworks-and-processes/change-is-easy-when-people-like-it-right.

Change management expert Daryl Conner presents this model as the emotional cycle of change when people first embrace it from a positive standpoint initially but resist it later. There's a good reason it looks like a roller coaster. In business and in life we experience some serious ups and downs!

Let's see how this model applies to your career journey.

People begin their changes full of hope and enthusiasm—partly because they don't realize how challenging the process will be. In the **Uninformed Optimism** phase, a person is envisioning how wonderful the change will feel when it's complete.

Then reality sets in. Shortly after starting, the challenges pile up and people get frustrated. They reach **Informed Pessimism**, the danger that comes with acquiring knowledge of the problems faster than knowledge of the solutions. This leads to **"checking out**," or withdrawing from the decision to change. This can take place in private or in public as the person regrets their initial hope and backpedals away from their dream.

This is when most people drop out. The reality is that the majority of people don't have the discipline or the systems in place to survive. But you're reading this book, which means you want to thrive and you know change is possible. You're dreaming of a better future, and you're determined to make it happen. That puts you ahead of the pack.

For people like you who make it through, the hard work eventually pays off. **Hopeful Realism** sets in as knowledge of solutions eventually catches up to knowledge of problems. Through trial and error, those survivors grasp success with their own two hands.

Informed Optimism comes next. Not only do you have the solutions, you also know they work. You've applied them enough times to know what patterns are consistent, how to navigate them, and how to deal with unexpected flare-ups. Your hope is not just based on finally learning what to do but on the knowledge that you can consistently get the results you want by applying your skills. Informed optimism is also called confidence. Remember earlier when I said people worry too much about measuring their own confidence? Here's your yardstick.

Completion is last. This is when you've fully realized your goal. And guess what? The graph leads straight into the next wave. You get to start the struggle all over again with your new goal! But the accumulated confidence builds and builds through each successive wave until the process becomes innate.

So what do we do with this information? A few takeaways:

- **Informed Pessimism** leads to **Hopeful Realism**, but it takes work. Don't give up when you're confronted with the problems. Look for the solutions.
- Everyone goes through this emotional cycle. Keep that in mind and don't feel like you're weird or deficient when you struggle. Everyone feels this at some time, and this is just your turn to feel it. The sine waves are something that happen. The amplitude will inevitably be high to start, but will grow smaller over time. Keep these realities in mind so it's easier to accept and move through them.
- Zero out your external expectations. It doesn't matter what other people think. You have already built what you need to get you to this point in life. And that means you can build what you need to take your next step.
- Being vulnerable isn't bad—you're human! In fact, we all are! It's OK to feel discouraged at the points on the chart. You can feel discouraged and frustrated whenever you like, and you know what? People will understand. But they also want to see you get back up. Which is a fancy way of saying . . .
- *Own* where you are right now. Remember that you've made it this far. Maybe you're struggling, and that's partly due to your own decisions. Owning your mistakes gives you the power to learn from them and fix them. Take ownership of where you are and make the decision to move forward. Hop on that next wave and ride it to success!

Training Yourself to Move Past the Fear of Change

Solving the fear problem involves six steps.

Step 1: Start with Root Causes

What exactly are you afraid of? Identify all of your trigger points and write them down. At the same time, write down anything you can think of that helps you push through those fears.

Maybe this anxiety stems from people in your life. We discussed how fear of judgement, fear of letting people down, and worrying what our family will say can hinder our efforts. If your biggest fear is being judged by others, contextualize what that means. What right do those people have to judge you? Why are they judging you? Why are they critical? What fears might they have that underlie their accidental sabotage? And why are you tempted to let them sabotage you without pushing back?

Maybe your fear is losing the prestige that comes with your role. Are you afraid of losing status? Giving up the bragging rights that come with your impressive title? Why is that status important to you? Is it more important than long-term success?

It could be that your environment or past experiences have shaped your worry and inhibitions. What were the outcomes that shaped those negative thoughts? It's valuable to talk to others who might have been part of these situations and who could help you diagnose what led to these takeaways. Make sure you aren't sabotaging yourself by not addressing old wounds and environmental factors. Control your own destiny; don't let it be decided for you by events out of your control.

If being open with others is a struggle for you, take the advice of Mark Metry, author of *Screw Being Shy: Learn How to Manage Social Anxiety and Be Yourself in Front of Anyone*. When he spoke on my podcast, Mark opened up about his own history of trauma and abuse. The key, he said, was to overcome the past behaviors formed around these old wounds in order to move forward with confidence. Mark encouraged listeners to get their personal issues resolved so they can look outward instead of inward. "If you want to go far, you've got to go deep."

Step 2: Figure Out Your Motivation

Are you more motivated by avoiding pain or by moving toward pleasure? People saturated with anxiety tend to think more about avoiding pain, because that's their focal point. If you find yourself constantly running damage control in advance as you catastrophize, you're probably a pain avoider.

And if avoiding pain is your bigger motivation, learn to use that to your advantage. Psychologist Dr. Mary Lamia has spent her career studying and encouraging emotional awareness. She also authored two books, *What Motivates Getting Things Done* and *The Upside of Shame*. In her words, emotions give us the octane to get things done. Emotions fuel our efforts, and yet they don't always feel good. But that's how they work. In other words . . .

Step 3: Harness Negative Feelings to Urgently Move Forward

If you focus on how disappointed your parents will be if you reject the traditional path, you may find yourself paralyzed. But focusing instead on how disappointed they'll be if you live a miserable life and never achieve satisfaction gives you the urgency you need to push through your hesitation.

Understanding why you feel the way you do lets you use those feelings to your advantage. This is crucial, according to Dr. Lamia. "We generally think that the best course of action is to suppress an emotion or ignore an emotion or to get rid of it rather than figure it out. People who can understand their emotions do have an advantage, especially in business."

You can't stop yourself from having feelings. But you can make them work for you.

In fact, I did an entire compilation podcast episode on how fear can be useful. Fear is fuel. Who believes that? The guests on that podcast, for starters. Maybe you've heard of them.

- Kareen Walsh, author and CEO of Revampologist
- Andy Musliner, founder and CEO of InRoad Toys
- Greg Johnston, creative strategist
- Will Choi, president and CEO of VerticalApps
- Dr. Mary Lamia herself

If harnessing the power of fear helped these successful leaders, it can help you too.

Step 4: Separate Your Perception of Reality from Reality Itself

You can start by questioning your feelings. Ask yourself why you believe what you do. What happens in life and what we often *think* happens in life aren't the same. Do you try to predict the future? Are you often wrong? Is your worrying actually keeping you safe? Or have you made the right choices at the right times in spite of your fear?

Ask yourself two big questions:

1. Where did you fail others?
2. Where did you fail yourself?

Search for objective answers here, not just feelings. When did you really, actually, truly fail? Was it born from hesitance and avoidance? Did you turn the failure around, or did you give up?

Take ruthless stock of your true history, not your perceived history. You need to weed out any and all unreasonable fears that may have been holding you back your entire life.

Once you've reached a place of reality, separated your fears from the truth, and come to grips with your own need for perfection, you reach . . .

Step 5: What If

To truly overcome your fears, you need to play out "what if." This is an intentional projection of events. Unlike catastrophizing, you're going to go through in advance what the most likely scenario will be. If you tend to focus on problems, pay special attention to positives.

The point of this exercise is to recognize the power you gain in making your own choices. By choosing your own path instead of taking the easy way out with avoidance, you gain control of your own life. To truly follow your compass, you need to build the courage to trust it.

What happens to you along the way is not nearly as important as how you react to what happens. You don't need the perfect plan, you just need the best plan you can come up with right now. You'll change and adapt as you go. Trust yourself. Use that fear to your advantage.

Michael Wilkinson, founder of Leadership Strategies, the number one facilitation training company in the United States, got a serendipitous start. His specialty is helping companies stop having endless meetings that accomplish nothing and getting tied up in meaningless analysis. For years, he did this for free. Then, one day, someone asked to become his client—a *paying* client. Everything changed that day. It wasn't something Michael ever considered until that point, as he was already on a path to becoming a partner at Ernst & Young, one of the world's leading professional service organizations. But he made that pivot to do what he loved.

You may disagree with yourself over what is the proper way forward. Bear in mind that the purpose of analyzing risk is not to stop all momentum but to target the next path with the best ratio of risk to reward. Life and business go on—whether you like it or not. You can freeze in place and let everyone else make all your decisions for you, or you can seize your opportunities, perfect or otherwise, and make adjustments along the way.

Start laying some structure for your own analysis. Give yourself a deadline to make a decision and keep in mind that you're looking for the best-fit choice, not the perfect choice.

Once you've confronted the possible negatives, visualized the positives, and made your choice, there's one final step to solve your fear problem.

Step 6: Commit to the Transition

Throw yourself into the decision and race down that path. The roller coaster is waiting. Embrace it! As you use your momentum to see you through the uphill climb, remember that the best part is still coming.

Along the way, you're going to be focusing on the small while thinking big. Celebrate the small victories to continue your positive momentum. Reward yourself for every success as you continue to grind. Those little wins lead to big wins.

Remember coach Dana Cavalea? Dana says that you build momentum by taking one step at a time and creating minivictories for yourself. You'll get that feeling of winning and your confidence will go up, which will all lead to self-satisfaction.

"Play the long game, stay consistent, chop chop away. If you are chopping every day, you'll be a winner in the end."

As you weather small disappointments and failures, learn from them. Build faith in yourself to be resourceful and resilient. Then celebrate your success in learning from the failures! These are important wins too. Even if it's just a hug and a pat on the back from someone who's proud of you, get the credit you deserve for overcoming your fears and setbacks.

Make a small promise to yourself—some goal or marker. Keep that promise by achieving it. Keep doing this. Eventually you'll learn to trust yourself.

Keeping the Right Mindset

The entire goal of this chapter is to teach you how to get in the right mindset to power through your fear.

You don't have to reduce all fear to zero, and the reality is that you won't. Fear will always be there, but it's about managing it and turning it into fuel that creates positive momentum. And you don't need to be the bravest person on earth. You just need the strength to overcome your fears during that initial difficult grind at the start of every new project. If you can stick with your goals even through the pessimistic spots, you'll succeed.

Bear in mind that you're more likely to succeed if you feel good about your success. This is called the addiction to movement and positive growth. If you see yourself thriving, even in little ways, it's so much easier to stay motivated. Strategic momentum is good and important for the overall plan, but harnessing your emotional mind and making it work for you is too powerful to ignore.

The flip side is, make sure you don't fall for the volume illusion. This happens when people do a ton of things that seem like they should add up into one big success. You may feel like you're accomplishing something, but in reality you're doing a lot of busywork. Just because it feels good doesn't mean it's good for you. Make sure your outcomes deserve the hard work you're investing.

When you feel worried, grab a trusted confidant (a family member, a mentor, etc.) and talk about the problem. Talk about the fear too. Get your feelings out and let the other person help you minimize the catastrophic thinking. Don't stew in your own misery alone. Utilize your support network and get that toxic fear out of your brain.

And one last word of advice before this chapter's exercise: When a problem seems too big, break it down into more manageable problems. You don't eat an elephant in one big gulp—it takes a thousand little bites!

Prepare for Change in Real Life

What commonly gets us stuck is the fear we face in doing something new or outside of our comfort zone. Understand what's driving the potential roadblocks that keep you from moving forward.

Exercise 1: Understanding Your Triggers

List out the everything from your plan that you feel the most fearful of starting (this could be a situation, a specific tactic you have to execute, or a task you have to do). Then pick the *one* that seems to be giving the greatest anxiety.

Write the top fear you identified in the first box below. Now let's identify where this top fear comes from by going through the questions below.

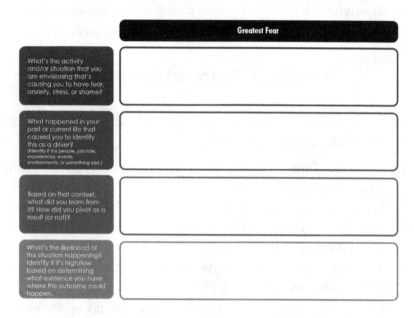

Exercise 2: Understand Your Risks and Rewards

Now list out the outcomes if you were to bring that activity/situation about which you have the most fear to life. Bucket them by positive outcomes versus negative ones like in the table below.

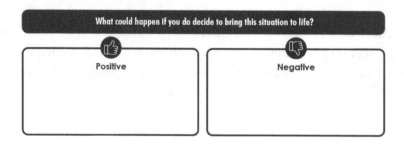

If the positives outweigh the negatives, then you know it's your fear and irrational thoughts that are inhibiting you from diving in. If the negatives outweigh the positives, you can choose not to follow through, but take note if you are only stopping to avoid near-term pain.

Exercise 3: Commit to Action

The following exercise is about helping you create a flywheel effect to build your psychological confidence.

1. Take one of the situations where you feel comfortable a positive outcome is likely based on what you did in parts 1 and 2.
2. Break down the activity/situation into all of its smaller parts that you'll need to execute to achieve your desired positive outcome.
   a. List out all the components.
3. Now circle the ones that give you the least amount of anxiety/nervousness with one color.
4. Circle the ones that give you the most amount of anxiety/nervousness with another color.
5. Group these activities into the three buckets:
   a. Low stress/anxiety based on what you circled in step 3
   b. Mid stress/anxiety (the rest that went uncircled)
   c. High stress/anxiety based on what you circled in step 4
6. Start tackling the activities that give you the lowest amount of stress first to start building momentum and confidence.

You'll find that the more you check off what you've done, the more confident you will become. These accomplishments will help you move toward tackling the activities that you've identified as high stress. Release the anxiety, and you're in an ideal position for what many consider the hardest step of the journey: networking.

CHAPTER 6

Networking
Your Way to
Implement Your Plan

Imagine you've got every aspect of your work life in perfect balance. You've studied *everything*. You know every move the market is going to make in the next six months. Your skills are sharpened to a razor's edge. And every skill set overlaps with the one before it, so you've become a towering stack of value. You've got your work life aligned to your personal values. Your compass points the way to your future. You've printed your career plan and hung it on your home office wall to inspire you. You may not know exactly where you'll be in five years, but you know how you'll feel about it—fulfilled.

Now what? Are you feeling stumped? How are you going to implement these plans? How do you advance? How do you get jobs?

I'll give you the answer: *people*. People are how you implement your plans. People are how you advance. People are how you get jobs.

Up until now, this book has been about the "what." What skills do I build? What do I focus on? What do I want to do with my work life?

Now we come to the "how." And that "how" in this case equals "who."

At the end of the day, people are going to help you find your next thing. People are behind the jobs and opportunities you need. It's not a computer that needs a job to be completed. It's not an app. It's a person.

The way to determine new opportunities is knowing the people who have insight into the jobs that to be done. These might be customers needing your skills, employers looking to build their company with new talent, or matchmakers who connect you to the people who are looking for you.

You've heard the old expression, "It's not what you know, it's who you know."

It's absolutely who you know. In this day and age, the people you know are a valuable source of data. They hold the crucial information you need to make connections and thrive in the new world of work. Not everything they know is captured online. It's not all ones and zeroes. It's more than raw data; it's the way you capture that data. By having a conversation with someone, you contextualize that data to you, your context, your needs, and your goals. The person you're speaking to shapes their conversation around your personal compass, which helps you elicit more information than a Google search could.

You might explain your compass to your conversation partner and ask, "Do you feel I'm on the right track? Am I doing what I need to do, building the skills that I need, and connecting with the people that I need to talk to?" You'll most likely gain real-time feedback on where you're at, how you're doing, and what you need to do next.

You're building the business of you. You are your own company, your own product, and your own CEO. You can't go anywhere without people. Networking is crucial to growing the business of you and fulfilling your purpose.

Does Networking Make You Nervous?

When networking comes up in discussion with friends, colleagues, or even those I mentor, the sentiment I often hear is that they know it's necessary but they don't necessarily like it. There tends to be a more negative perception around it because of all the transactional interactions many had in the past during "networking events." Yes, networking is hard. It makes a lot of people nervous. Some days, I too wished I could have just put my head down, done my job, and never bothered with watercooler talk. Not everyone is a social butterfly with an endless supply of bubbly positivity. Networking can be challenging—harder for some than for others.

But if you don't have a village, you don't have a chance in the new world of work. I learned this early in my career, and for that I am still exceedingly grateful. And there are some myths in building the right village for you. So I'm going to show you a simple, focused method for cultivating meaningful work and even personal relationships. You'll learn and follow this process, and before you know it, you'll be thriving in spite of any nervousness.

Remember when we discussed pushing through fear? This is crucial in networking.

The foundation always comes before the house. Before you can jump into successful networking, you'll need to lay a networking foundation. Have you heard of the seven Ps? "Proper prior planning prevents piss-poor performance."

If you're struggling with insecurity, I'll show you how to deliver consistent value to your network so you earn every piece of advice you get. Networking relationships are a two-way exchange of guidance and insight. I'll also show you how to do that thing we all dread so much: *ask for help*.

It's OK if you're not perfect at this right away. Networking is an ongoing process. The more comfortable you become with reaching out to others, the easier it gets.

Keeping Realistic Expectations

While some people imagine networking as a slow and painful crawl, others imagine sprinting out to the next social gathering and flinging themselves into exciting conversations. We all feel differently about engaging in social interaction. And whether you're picturing a crawl or a sprint, neither is correct. Cultivating your network is a marathon. You shouldn't rush ahead, burn yourself out, and alienate people. Taking on fifty new friends in a week is a sure way to fail to meet any of your obligations to them. But dreading your social experiences may keep you from forming any connections at all. Both pathways will keep you stuck without the quality networking connections you need.

Picture your network growing over months, years, and decades. You may not have the connections you need for that perfect job right now, but with a little networking (and building the *skill* of networking) you may see a hundred new open doors in just a year's time. You don't have to rush out and become best friends with everyone at your current company. You simply need a strategic guide to connect with two or three people who can help you step up to that next level you've been eyeing.

Like with everything else we've covered so far, networking is about starting small, testing, and learning along the way. There's no pressure to get it right on the first try. Remember when we removed the fear of failure in the last chapter? You can't get this wrong either.

Your networks will change on their own over time. People will retire, have kids and drop out, or take a new job in Alaska. Your closest ally today may advance in their own career path tomorrow, and you may completely lose touch with them. And your own goals are going to change continuously over your lifetime. Your network should change continuously to reflect that.

Your network is not about finding one friend and sticking to them like glue for the rest of your life. It's also not about finding three hundred new friends and shoving your business card aggressively into their hands so they're grateful when you move on to your next victim. Relax and breathe into it. Get comfortable at your own pace. This will let you learn what works for you and what doesn't. The approaches that feel the most natural will bring you the best results.

You may have heard that it takes a village to raise a child. Your work life is your child, and you're building a village to raise it. In fact, you're going to build multiple villages in every different industry, so that no matter where your child goes, it's got a network to help it thrive.

Dispelling the Myths and Misconceptions

People have some really funny ideas about networking. They imagine all kinds of horrible and unrealistic scenarios. Since you already know how to overcome your fears and stop catastrophic thinking through the application of reality, let's poke holes in your perception of networking and get you on the right track.

It's Not Just Who You Know, It's Who *They* Know

Professionals just learning to network often believe their first-degree connections are most likely the ones to help them get to where they want to go. This is a natural assumption, to assume your closest associates have your best interests at heart because they know you. Many of us believe we'll gain traction faster with our first-degree connections because they know us and know our work.

The bad news is that these assumptions are flawed. Just because these connections know us doesn't mean they are going to immediately act on our behalf. There is an inherent selfish versus service mentality with your first-degree connections. "Me" in most cases still comes before "we." Self-preservation and self-interest is primal, particularly if you work in the same field or industry.

Another thing is that these first-degree connections are more likely to already know what we do, so they don't expand our information or even our network—particularly if you are looking to make a pivot into another industry.

Now that you understand this flawed thinking, you can adapt your approach.

The way to create a network that really works for you is to have the right mindset and approach from the start. It's about playing the long game, not the short one. It's not one and done. This means you're going to plug a lot of time into growing connections, which involves expanding outside of your immediate connections into their direct networks—those second-degree connections.

They travel in different social circles and work at different companies or even industries. As a result, they'll know different people, information, and resources than your close relationships. The goal is not about soliciting opportunities from the first-degree connections but expanding to the second-degree connections for these very reasons.

Plus, these second-degree connections won't view you through the lens of what you've done or where you've been in the past like your first-degree connections. Ironically, those who know you best may not be able to truly see you in a new and different way because their reference point is from the past. You'll always be subconsciously known as the eager yet quiet data analyst rather than the vocal, confident marketing director who you've become.

Second-degree connections don't have that baggage. They will know you for who you are now and where you want to go. We also have more to learn from the people that we don't already know so well. That's a wealth of new knowledge and perspective you haven't encountered.

And sometimes, the best person to advocate for you is someone who doesn't know you that well.

Advancing connections is the main game!

And keep in mind that the network effect is maximized when you have a service mentality rather than a selfish mentality. Focus on helping anyone with whom you get connected and deliver value. They'll want to help you out in turn. Paying it forward by always helping will pay itself back in spades.

It's Not Transactional, It's Relational

Sometimes we picture networking like one of those movies about stereotypical 1980s businessmen: a room full of professionals angling to find the best way to exploit each other to maximize their own gain, even if it hurts the people they're connecting with.

That's not at all what I'm teaching. If that's how you network, you're doing it wrong. You may see some short-term gain, but people will quickly identify you as an exploitative and selfish person who gives nothing back. Nobody wants that reputation.

Instead, feel at ease with the knowledge that you don't need to be ruthless and cutthroat. You aren't out to exploit anyone. You're going to be building genuine relationships with the people around you based on mutual satisfaction and mutual gain. As you help their career, they'll help yours. If you and your new friend are each running "the business of you," you'll be building your companies together.

Jordan Harbinger encourages professionals to remember ABG: "always be giving" or "always be generous." The key to building authentic relationships, says Jordan, is to provide value to others without counting the points and demanding compensation. Focus on providing constant value to others, and they will naturally return the favor with interest.

In other words, focus on taking care of the people around you, and they'll take care of you.

It's Not Just Who You Know, It's How You Invest in Them

Here's a clarification on what I said earlier. You may know the perfect people and have the perfect network of six hundred contacts. But if you're aggressively gathering names like an autograph collector, no one is going to want to help you.

Relationships grow based on time and attention. If you're not cultivating individual relationships with time and attention, they're going to remain small and unhelpful. You need to invest time in relationships just as you do in your skills. Both will help you advance on your career path, and both are absolutely irreplaceable. If the choice for a promotion comes down to you and a candidate the boss eats lunch with every day, you'll be out in the cold.

It's Not about How Hard It Feels, It's about Exercising Yourself

People without a natural gift for social exuberance often worry they'll never be able to succeed at networking. They imagine it's a talent you're either born with or without. They think it's all or nothing and sink into defeat before they even begin. Nothing could be further from the truth.

Networking is a skill you can learn, just like any other. That skill becomes stronger the more you work at it. If you start lifting weights today for the first time in your life, are you going to be able to break the world record before dinner? Not a chance. In fact, you'll probably feel exhausted and sore tomorrow.

If you stopped and declared you'd never be able to lift anything bigger than that first weight, your friends would laugh at your naivete. They might shout something encouraging like, "Just keep going! It gets easier as you get stronger! Don't give up right at the start, because you're at your weakest point!"

Apply the same thinking to your networking skills. You're not going to break any records on your first day. You don't need the whole room hanging on your every word. Start small and build your muscles.

Let me clarify something. COVID-19 has *not* made networking impossible. In some ways, it's easier than ever! You've got a captive audience now. People are stuck at home or in a lonely, sterile office. They crave human interaction. You're actually at an advantage when you offer them a few minutes to speak to another person without feeling isolated.

Contrary to popular belief, the time has never been better to cultivate strong networks.

Creating the Connections to New Opportunities

Now that your fears are dispelled or, at the very least, held at bay, let's talk about the proven pathway you're going to follow to build a valuable network.

Networking is a three-step process:

1. Assessing and mapping your network
2. Building the operational path
3. Making it real

We'll walk through each of these until you're ready to act. By the end of this chapter, you'll have a clear plan for how to proceed with confidence.

Assessing Your Networking

To understand what you need to do, identify where you're starting. Your first step is to take an objective assessment of your current network. These are your first-degree connections. You're going to bring your village to life by cataloguing every person you know who can help you, both personally and professionally.

Yes, friends and family can be a major asset too. Begin by listing your personal friends and family who may have some helpful work connections, industry connections, or who just know useful people you might need down the line.

A lot of people who aren't comfortable with networking start with close friends and family. There is absolutely nothing wrong with this. The only issue is if they don't venture out beyond their personal circles.

But don't limit yourself solely to those you see on a daily basis. Also note your professional connections. Old bosses, former coworkers, vendors you've worked with, people you've helped, and mentors you may have lost touch with. Think through all of your professional relationships across your career. If you have precious few, take note of that. It may be that you've spent no time at all cultivating relationships in your work life, or you've never thought to ask for contact information before someone leaves. That's something you can learn to fix.

Arrange your first-degree connections according to high, medium, and low alignment with your goals, objectives, and interests. This may lead to some surprising or even uncomfortable realizations about some of your connections, but don't worry if your mom gets placed in low alignment. This isn't a chart to document how important these people are to you, just how well they can help you along your career path at the moment.

Now that you've got your network assessed and mapped, you're ready for the real magic: expansion.

Building the Operational Path

Your next step is to research your network's network. You're going to map out the people around each one of your first-degree connections. These are your second-degree connections, also called loose connections. Loose connections also sprout off this map into third-degree connections when you map out the people connected to your second-degree connections.

By the time you're done, you'll have a sprawling web of human beings with tagged value to your goals, objectives, and interests.

Then you ask your first-degree connections to make the introductions. You meet their network, and those new people become your contacts. Having a warm contact like this increases the likelihood of successful connecting versus cold contact over LinkedIn. And if you do get a chance to meet these second-degree contacts, make sure you do your research on them before you meet them!

Remember our seven *P*s: "Proper prior planning prevents piss-poor performance." Research helps guide your communications and engagement and reduces the likelihood of coming across as transactional. Get to know their background and interests, such as:

- where they've worked (or where they are working)
- what they've done
- what do they do outside of work

Identify potential information or even people who could be useful to them based on their interests. This is how you can plan to add value to these current and potential new contacts. Your intention is to find and cultivate commonality to create an authentic connection. That means building solid rapport and drawing these new connections into your circle.

What's fascinating about networking is that your *loose connections* might be your best advocates. Loose connections are second-degree connections, meaning they are people that your network knows but you don't. Your loose connections will often be the best thing that ever happened to your career. Many times the people who know you the least end up helping you get to where you want to go. This often happens because they're also in networking mode. By identifying useful loose connections and tightening them up by spending time on those relationships, you are networking. Your mother may not be able to walk into a CEO's office and explain why you're the best candidate for the job. But someone who knows you a little bit, and who also knows the CEO, is often happy to make that connection between you with just a little bit of encouragement on your part.

Your loose connections also aren't biased based on what you've done before. They may see your potential to grow in new directions instead of keeping you stuck in a labeled box. They're more likely to recommend new things to you, like growth opportunities that people who know you best might not even think of. Now, they may not be willing to make a recommendation for you out of the blue. Have lunch and explain yourself first. And don't worry, you'll learn a formula for how to do that later in the chapter.

As you list your various connections, remember to ask yourself, "Who do I know, even a little bit, with a connection to a new industry I want to pivot into? Or who knows someone with loose connections to that industry?"

Loose connections, sometimes known as weak ties, also contribute to social and emotional well-being. Your network is not simply everyone you already know. The second-degree connections are everything. A recent study found that the more loose ties a person has, the happier they feel.[42] This informal network of casual acquaintances contributes to a sense of belonging and community. There is potential for branching out and converting second-degree connections into first-degree relationships who are able to bring you to the next stage of your career journey.

Feels like a lot right now, doesn't it? That's OK. The business of you is dynamic and free-flowing. It's one thing at a time, and it's everything all at once. Fluid work is bidirectional work. So is networking. You pour into other people's lives, and you receive back from them. That's authentic networking. Over the near-term future, you'll begin to leverage your personal, professional, and loose connections into a large web. Strengthening those connections means you can start connecting to your connections' connections. You can then make several new loose connections through them. Your connections are like seeds that can grow

---

42   Gillian M. Sandstrom and Elizabeth W. Dunn, "Social Interactions and Well-Being: The Surprising Power of Weak Ties," Personality and Social Psychology Bulletin (2014), https://doi.org/10.1177/0146167214529799.

into deeper relationships, and those seeds are sprinkled all around you. All you have to do is recognize the opportunities they represent and help them grow. Your network is not simply everyone you already know. The second-degree connections are everything. In business development, this is called referral marketing or word of mouth. A friend of a friend tells a friend of a friend of a friend. Then someone makes a sale; someone gets a job.

When you realize the power of loose connections, you want to continually nurture everyone you know in real life. So build those relationships. *Invest.* Reach out to the connections you already have and ask some questions. Get their input on who you should be talking to. Maybe you don't know much about the big names in your desired industry, but you might have a loose connection who has all the inside information. Leverage that connection to help figure out who else to talk to. And who knows? Maybe your loose connection can get you a meeting that everyone else has been dying to get.

This isn't about pitching, it's about value. Someone you know, like, and trust can vouch for you and you for them. That goes a long way. Nielsen found that 92 percent of people worldwide trust recommendations from family, friends, and colleagues above *any* form of advertising.[43] Remarkable—what someone says about you goes much further than anything you can tell someone about yourself.

What you're essentially doing is melding your research with your networking. The research becomes the guide, and the networking is the resulting action. Your research shows you who to talk to, and your networking gets you the connections you need to achieve your next goal.

Once you've figured out all the second- and third-degree connections you're looking to build, it's time to assemble a standard script. I'll elaborate on specifically how to do this in the next section. You're going to put together a simple message you can tailor to each professional you want to contact. Keep in mind that you need to avoid the use of "I"

---

43 "Consumer Trust in Online, Social and Mobile Advertising Grows," Neilsen, April 11, 2012, www.nielsen.com/us/en/insights/article/2012/consumer-trust-in-online-social-and-mobile-advertising-grows/.

statements to prevent coming off as selfish. Focus on your introduction to them instead. Remember that less is more. You don't always need six paragraphs here, maybe just a few targeted sentences. More elaborate circumstances may require a bit more, but no one wants a book sprung on them, so you should focus on front-loading the message with the important pieces. First and foremost, deliver context and value, specifically, who you know in common and what you can do for them. This is especially important if this person isn't a first-degree contact.

This script can help streamline the entire process down the line and is especially useful in the next step.

When you understand who you need to talk to, why, and how, effective networking is easy. And any discomfort felt along the way is worth it. Because as HR consultant Olivia Gamber says, "Your success in life and business is a product of the relationships you have. Whatever you are trying to achieve, you will get there faster by leveraging your network."[44] Here's how.

Making it Real

When it's time to make those connections, tailor your script to the person you're contacting. There are a few ways to do this, and there are some common mistakes to avoid.

Provide the context for your outreach. You need to state the purpose of your contact right up front so they're not wondering what this is about.

Do your research on them first so you know a bit about them. Then work on getting to know them a little bit better before you make a request of them. That may mean your request comes at the very end of the conversation. People don't like strangers making demands, but they're usually happy to help someone who brightens their day with a friendly conversation. Even if your request is for this connection to help

---

44   Jeff Boss, "4 Ways To Uncover the Power of 2nd and 3rd Degree Connections in Your Network," Forbes, July 20, 2015, www.forbes.com/sites/jeffboss/2015/07/20/4-ways-to-uncover-the-power-of-2nd-and-3rd-degree-connections-in-your-network/?sh=1f3be63c3b97.

make an introduction to someone else, spend the time talking with them and making it feel organic.

Ask what you can do for them. Don't make the entire conversation about your desires. This can be especially important in those first-degree connections where selfish concerns may exist, and they may be hesitant to share the contacts they're hoping to leverage for their own future opportunities. Providing value and help to the person may encourage them to open up and share more generously. Provide suggestions along the way that may prove useful to them.

When you reach out to someone, don't say something like, "I want to pick your brain." This sounds entirely transactional. You're trying to get information for free. Even if you're offering to pay for their time, you're really just buying a service from them.

That's not a relationship. Instead, try saying something like,

- "I'd love to hear your advice."
- "I'd love to get your thoughts."
- "Your insight and guidance would be tremendously valuable."

The phrasing here makes these requests more relational than transactional. They make it clear that you value the other person. You aren't just there to grab data and run. You respect them, and you're looking for their personal thoughts and input.

It's also crucial that you thank them for their time. Reaching out to someone on a higher playing field than your current position means they're doing you a favor by responding. Odds are, they're spending valuable time they could be using on something else and answering your question instead. Be authentically grateful for that. Preface your response to their answer with, "Thank you for taking the time to explain that to me." You can even thank them in advance at the end of your opening message.

Your first introduction to someone should follow the so-called sandwich method:

- Open with context and value. Explain why you're contacting them and who you are. Compliment them as you do so.
- Explain the connection between you two. Tell them what people join the two of you and how your networks connect.

- Close with a compliment and a thank you. Leave them with a positive feeling on the very last word.

It is crucially important to catch your recipient's attention right away. Erin King, founder of Socialite Agency and best-selling author of *Digital Persuasion: Sell Smarter in the Modern Marketplace* hammers this point. Your recipient receives constant emails and offers all day long, and they're packed with the same niceties. Erin urged listeners to cut the niceties and instead focus on grabbing attention right away with something personal, something the recipient actually cares about, so they stop the mindless scroll to actually read your words.

Compliments are an easy way to get this attention, because every human being loves to hear genuine praise for their accomplishments. But keep the compliments believable, not flattering. You don't want to open with, "You're the smartest person in the whole industry!" That falls flat and makes it blatantly obvious you're just buttering them up to get something out of them. Instead try saying something complimentary about their work. "That piece you wrote last month was really insightful and got me thinking about a new aspect of the industry I'd overlooked." This is more targeted toward their work and their intelligence, and it reaffirms their value. It also shows that you've paid attention to their specific contributions and have done some research on them, which shows they have your attention and makes you seem more genuine.

Following these steps might get you a message that reads something like this:

> John, your most recent blog post about networking really blew me away. I've been studying networking and have a new idea that touches on your concept, and I would love to get your thoughts on it. Sophia, who spoke at the networking conference last month, suggested you might find it useful in your own work. Thank you in advance for your time. I know your educated input would be tremendously valuable.

And then, please, please, please follow up. This means so much and shows that you're really interested. Sometimes the big names won't see your first message, or they may even wait to see if you push a second time to make sure you're serious about making the connection. If they do respond, don't leave them hanging. Respond back and set up a time to connect.

And after you've talked with them, follow up again. Send an immediate thank you for their time and valuable input. Reiterate how their conversation was helpful to you. Inform them you intend to send a LinkedIn connection. Convey what you promised to do in your last conversation and how you will help them. Then close with a statement of support for their own endeavors.

- "I'm in your corner."
- "Love to see you kill it."
- "I'm rooting for you."
- "Want to follow your progress on that interesting project."

Remember, this is about building trusting relationships. You need to be authentic. Don't spout useless flattery just to butter someone up, and don't go over the top with your compliments if you don't really feel them. You also don't want to go promising enormous value to people if you can't produce results. Notice my example didn't say, "My new idea is going to change your life forever." Keep yourself honest and people are far more likely to respond positively.

How Big of a Network Do You Need?

The answer depends completely upon your goal. The real dynamic here is one of breadth versus depth. If you want to be a social influencer, you're going to need a lot of connections. In fact, one could say that your business is almost entirely about connections. You'll become the connecting point between customers and solutions. This means you'll spend the bulk of your networking time growing new connections, meeting new people, and figuring out what makes all the pieces of society move the way they do. An influencer needs to focus more on the breadth of their social network.

However, if your focus is on finding new jobs, new revenue streams, and new launching points for yourself, you'll need better relationships. You need to be the first person people think of. Depth will be your primary focus in networking. This means you'll be spending the bulk of your networking time cultivating relationships that already exist and making sure they're solid and mutually beneficial for the other person. A job seeker needs to focus more on the depth of their network.

Now, this is not an excuse to ignore either side. You don't want to build a lake a thousand miles wide and one inch deep. You also don't want a single well that plunges to the earth's core. An influencer can't influence without some genuine depth, and a job seeker needs more than a single resource to find a range of opportunities. Ideally, you cultivate both. You just *specialize* into breadth or depth according to your need.

And if your need changes down the line, if you shift from job seeker to influencer, then you change your approach from depth to breadth. That's another reason not to focus on just one aspect and ignore the other. Your networking needs may change as you go.

The best answer is to build the network you need right now without narrowing yourself toward getting stuck in the future. Give yourself enough breadth *and* depth to move around and stay fluid. The last thing you want is to be forced to halt everything in your life and cultivate new relationships from scratch because you didn't network enough.

Measuring Success: The Networking Edition

Network measuring can be extremely difficult. You can't just count up the number of people you know, and you can't rest on having two best friends. Numbers don't give a clear picture of effectiveness here.

But we all need markers to tell us how we're doing. Until you get a comfortable feel for the ebb and flow of networking, you're going to wonder if you've done enough.

The best way to tell is tracking your own tangible milestones. Are you accomplishing changes that you want to see? Have you pivoted in the direction of your compass? Are you earning more? Are you getting more time with your family? Are you feeling more fulfilled?

Ask yourself, "How did networking help me succeed in reaching my tangible milestones?" Who helped you along the way? Did you leverage relationships to make the changes you wanted? Did you fall short of reaching a goal because you didn't know the right people?

Keep track of how your relationships either grow you or limit you. Where you feel limited, you need to do work. If you're flying through the green lights and every door seems open, you can be confident that you're doing a good job of networking.

The easiest way to measure your networking is through your results. Are you where you want to be? Then you're networking the right way for your needs.

Along the way, keep something in mind: networking isn't some magical switch you flip on and off. Every conversation you have can be a networking exercise. It may be as simple as getting your tired colleague a cup of coffee, asking an accountant to lunch, or taking stress off your boss's plate so she can get to her kid's soccer game. Networking doesn't have to be crafty and strategic; it can just happen in everyday life.

And it's never about counting up points. I told you before that networking is relational, not transactional, and I absolutely meant that. As my friend (and networking ninja) Dan Yu always says, *never count points*. You'll be absolutely miserable. Either you'll come out ahead and become resentful of the other person, or they'll come out ahead and you'll feel insecure.

Networking is not about what you can do for the other person or what they can do for you. Networking is all about connecting your two networks to help each other thrive. By connecting your two networks, you build one giant network. Connecting to a third network creates a supernetwork. Sometimes it's not about who you know, it's about who you know who knows someone else you need to meet. And returning the favor back to them builds a positive circle where everyone succeeds. That makes them more likely to want to help you in the future.

Marc Angelos, CEO of Anvictus and relationship management expert, knows this truth. He teaches how to build true rapport—at the end of the day, it's about a value exchange, Marc basically told me. If I've brought you value, you'll bring me the connection I'm seeking with you. But if I'm just looking for connection and there's no value trade, you're not interested in that.

In other words, remember to provide value to the other person in exchange for what you're getting. After all, the interaction doesn't cost you anything; they're spending their precious time talking with you! Make sure you're providing some sort of value.

Authenticity is key here. Don't sit around thinking about how to use someone for their connections and then drop them like a rock. Ladder climbers leave a lot of hurt feelings in their wake, and word gets around. Be grateful to the people who've helped you in the past, because they may know someone much bigger than you who could help you in the future.

Learn to give value to your network by asking people things like:

- "How can I help you?"
- "What's the burning question you're trying to solve these days?"
- "What's most pressing to you?"

People will see how unselfish you are. They may be insecure and nervous about asking for help, but by offering, you help them break through their struggles and reach their success. That creates gratitude. It also creates a strong ally to help you along your career path. You become two businesses working side by side in the new world of work, sharing resources so that both thrive.

And keep in mind that networking is not just empty friend making and bridge building. Networking can teach you how to cultivate new skills you've been missing, both hard and soft, skills you'll need five steps down the line to reach your ultimate goals. Networking can provide all the answers to those burning questions that keep you up at night and fill in all the missing pieces of your puzzle.

Just remember to provide value to the people around you, be grateful to those who help you, and never stop building your network.

Networking to Implement Your Plan: Exercise

Your strategic plan takes people to help you get there. The following exercises will help identify your village of support based on your interests as well as how to build real connections with them that can lead to a sustainable and mutually beneficial relationship—all to guide you in the near and long term.

Network Assessment: Create Your Hierarchy of Career Relationships

Make a list of the most important people in your personal life with family at the top. Identify which ones align in terms of their background, interests, and experience to what you want to do in your strategic plan. Then categorize them as low, medium, or high by how aligned they are. Look to engage those connections who are highly aligned with what you want to do first.

List of Personal Relationships	Alignment to Interests, Activities with Your Strategic Plan (High, Med, Low)
Nuclear family, parents, children, siblings	
Aunts and uncles, cousins, grandparents, grandchildren	
Best friends	
Acquaintances	
Neighbors	
All the way at the bottom, that 7th cousin you haven't spoken to in years	

Now make a list of key people in your professional life. Reach out to those who are at the top of your hierarchy and align to your interests and activities first, then go down to those who are lower in the hierarchy yet still align to your interests.

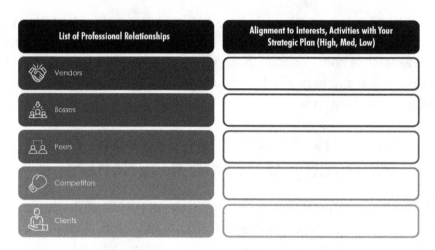

List of Professional Relationships	Alignment to Interests, Activities with Your Strategic Plan (High, Med, Low)
Vendors	
Bosses	
Peers	
Competitors	
Clients	

Clients should be at the bottom. Why? If you provide an honest service for a good price, they will probably come back. However, if you change firms, or maybe even industries, those clients may not be in a position to help you with your career. Put them at the bottom.

Above your clients, put your employees or the team that support you. They make you look good to your clients.

Above them, put your peers. They will have your back when you need to take a vacation or when you're involved with something else and something needs attention. One day, they may advance and be a decision maker for your job or career.

Above them, put your bosses, because they will have a more strategic view of the industry, and conversely, their bosses should go above them. This will give you a "canary-in-a-coal-mine" viewpoint. This shouldn't replace your own research but rather supplement it.

And at the top, put vendors and competitors. They will have their own viewpoint of the industry, and they will definitely supplement your research efforts.

Now we want to identify potentially valuable second-degree connections based on the contacts you have identified. Here are a few steps for doing just that.

1. List out your goals, interests, and activities/tactics based on your strategic plan.
2. Use LinkedIn to search your personal and professional contact's network.
3. Filter by companies, titles, industries, skills and interests.
4. Who comes up? What does their profile tell you?

Research your contacts' lists of potential connections for people you might want to be introduced to based on how they align to your goals and interests.

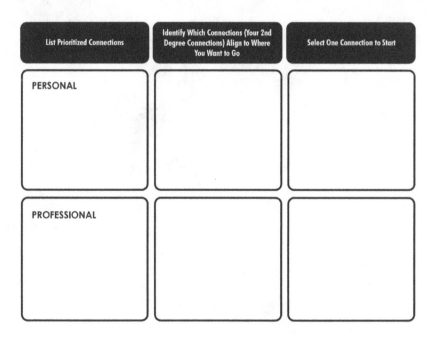

Preparation is crucial before you reach out to any of your contacts. Why? Because without preparation, you run the risk of not coming across as purposeful, focused, and polished.

Your likelihood of getting your current connections (and definitely new potential connections) to help you on your career journey is going to be severely challenged if you can't clearly articulate what you are looking for in a way that is genuine. The last thing you want to do is waste anyone's time.

Doing this homework is worth it. The bigger the village, the more potential opportunities for you to add value to individuals, companies, and the people who work for them. But wait a minute. What if you aren't confident in your skill sets? What if you've got gaps you're struggling to close?

You might say that we've saved the best for last. And we have. Coming up next, skill building to go from learning to mastery—even for skills you need to complete your mashup but don't yet have. Let's go!

CHAPTER 7

Building Your Hard and Soft Skills

You've learned quite a bit over the last several chapters. Pause for a moment and take it all in. To begin, you learned how to map the lay of the land. Next came your compass, the master blueprint toward your goals. After that you built your plans. You learned to manage and even leverage your fear so you're no longer limited by emotions. And now you're equipped to be a master in the art of networking. You have nearly everything you need to succeed in the new world of work. The missing piece of the puzzle is now building your skills!

Bosses will like that you have plans, but plans don't get the job done. And networking is fantastic to get your foot in the door, but the next step is making a lasting impression. Having the right skills means you become a valuable member of the team for years to come. The whole system hinges on the skills you build and prepare yourself to apply in a work setting. Put simply, skills pay the bills.

As you build your skill sets, you prepare yourself to get jobs done. The wider the range of jobs you can perform, the more valuable you become to companies. Mastering your current skills and learning new ones moves you forward from planning to execution. This is where you apply everything you've learned in this book so far.

If skills are so essential, why does the skills chapter come at the end of the list? Why didn't we start with skills? Too many people jump straight to execution without adequate planning. You really need to complete the first four phases before you take your leap. Poor planning and frenzied execution may be exactly what led you to this book, searching for a way out of your current system. Take the time to do the work in the correct order, and the process to build these news skills becomes innate.

Spotting the trends is research, and creating your compass is planning which hard skills will be needed to make the most of those trends. In this chapter, we'll explore the best ways for you to cultivate those hard skills and also cultivate soft skills. It's all part of execution.

Emotional Quotient (EQ)

Much fuss has been made over something called EQ. Executives rave about it. Consultants pound the desk praising its virtue. Most agree it plays a key role in personal success. But very few people have a firm grasp on what it is and why it's so crucial.

What is EQ?

When asked to define EQ, most people will give you a list of examples.

- "It's knowing what people want."
- "It's about good communication."
- "It's reading the room."
- "It's about making sure you're not coming off like a weirdo."

Most people struggle to define EQ, and for good reason. It's extremely nebulous. It can't be easily measured, but its absence is definitely felt. The most scientific explanation is to say that just as intelligence quotient

(IQ) measures a person's ability to learn hard skills, emotional quotient (EQ) is a strong predictor of a person's soft skills. And the good news is, EQ can be taught.

Even that's still abstract, isn't it? EQ is more than social skills because you also use it on yourself. It's more than knowledge of psychology because it's not clinical. It isn't only communication skills, because you can display it with action and not speak a word.

"Connie, this is too vague! Can't you just give me a simple explanation?"

A useful definition of EQ I've arrived at is this: EQ is awareness of how people act (including yourself), why they act that way, what the consequences are, and what to do about it. As a result, EQ helps you navigate situations with other humans and achieve success.

Applied to ourselves, Travis Bradbury, author of *Emotional Intelligence 2.0*, calls this **personal competence.** It's the ability to stay aware of your emotions and manage your behavior and tendencies. This breaks down into two components:

- **Self-Awareness:** Perceiving your own emotions accurately.
- **Self-Management:** Adjusting your own behavior based on that perception.

As leadership coach and Initiate Consulting founder Joanie Rufo knows, you can't lead others until you learn to lead yourself. If you don't understand yourself, and if you aren't managing yourself with compassion and understanding, you will fail at managing others. You're not a manager right now and don't plan on becoming one? Not so fast. Personnel management is an essential skill even for gig workers, many of whom end up hiring subcontractors. In Joanie's words, you are the first organization you must master. Sounds a lot like prioritizing the business of you, doesn't it?

Reflect, check in, and ground yourself. That's a luxury many of us don't think we can take. But it's absolutely crucial that we make the time to do this. Running yourself into exhaustion means decreasing your own compassion reservoir for those who rely on you. And who wants to work for or with someone who seems absolutely miserable all the time?

Think about working on yourself as practice for working with others. The same understanding and compassion you apply on yourself to get positive results will give excellent data on how to get positive results out of others. When applied to others, Bradbury calls this **social competence.** It's the ability to understand people's moods, behaviors, and motives to improve relationship quality. This also breaks down into two components:

- **Social Awareness:** Perceiving other people's emotions accurately.
- **Relationship Management:** Managing interactions with others based on that perception.

But how important is EQ in a work setting?

The Importance of EQ

Picture a smooth, perfect office space. Everyone is friendly. People resolve their concerns quickly and without angry words. Everyone is helpful to each other, everyone gets their job done on time, and then everyone departs to their happy home to get rested and refreshed for the next day.

Now imagine the opposite. Everyone is grumpy. People don't solve their problems—they let them fester until they're shouting and resentful, or they even sabotage each other. Everyone is suspicious and refuses to help anyone else. Jobs don't get done on time because people are stressed and angry. They head home miserable, where they meet more misery from unhappy family members who don't welcome this thundercloud hanging over their head. They come in the next morning just as grumpy as the day before.

What's wrong here? No hard skills are missing. Every employee has the tools and skills they need to accomplish their work. But they don't have leadership that understands good EQ and how to apply it. EQ helps leaders and employees understand how crucial it is to keep their team working together like a well-oiled machine. Without EQ:

- People don't work together for mutual gain but seek to exploit others.
- People make hurtful comments and don't realize the impact.
- People act ungrateful for the work others do.
- People don't consider how their own gaps may negatively impact others.

A lack of EQ means there's a million things in the way of simply doing your job. If you're a leader, it's your job to be aware of these challenges and resolve them so the team can work smoothly. If you're an employee, simply modeling good EQ for your coworkers and managers can have an impact. And if you're an entrepreneur, you can use good EQ to build and maintain high-quality relationships with clients, contractors, and anyone else you come in contact with.

EQ can be the difference between a company thriving or collapsing. Workers with a high-EQ leader may dominate an industry, while workers with a low-EQ leader may be seen as the disaster of the industry. Even if you struggle to define EQ, you do *not* want to be known for lacking it. Sites like Glassdoor are full of brutal reviews of low-EQ workers and leaders who ran their coworkers and employees into the ground without regard for their well-being.

On a special *Strategic Momentum* episode, we brought on several guests to discuss the heavy impact of EQ in the workplace. The takeaway was simple: *EQ is not optional*. It's absolutely essential if you want to keep your job and navigate the company politics. EQ has an incredible impact on your professional success. It's the single biggest predictor of performance in the workplace and the strongest driver of leadership and excellence. It's what turns all those hard skills into consistent positive results without chaos. It helps you see what's going on in relationships and enables you to establish and maintain relationships more effectively.

Now that you understand how important EQ is, let's talk about how it makes up a significant portion of your soft skills.

What Are Soft Skills?

Soft skills, generally speaking, are the personal habits and traits that shape how you work on your own and with others.[45] Some soft skills are simply the application of EQ. You use your basic understanding of behavior, apply it to a negative consequence you want to avoid, then build a pathway around that negative consequence to reach a positive one.

Before reading this book, you might not have known exactly what you wanted out of your professional life. You may have been drifting or felt lost or frustrated. The fear might have been that you'd end up in retirement with half your dreams unfinished and a lifetime of regret. You wanted to avoid this, so you defined your goals. You also built a compass to keep you directed straight toward those goals for the rest of your life. You've met with people and learned how to engage with them in an authentic way while also overcoming those deep-seated fears that could have limited any forward progress on your plan in the first place. In doing this, you cultivated deeper EQ about your own behavior and then applied that EQ with several soft skills.

Before reading this book, you might have struggled to execute plans because worry held you back. You looked ahead and realized that letting your fears run the show would leave you miserable and unfulfilled. You acknowledged that problem and found a way around it by making your fear work for you. You stopped your catastrophic thinking by applying reality. In doing this, you raised an important dimension of your EQ and applied it through more soft skills (defining concerns, problem-solving, and reality checking).

Your other soft skills may be personal characteristics you pride yourself on. Perhaps they're helpful mindsets or behaviors you've picked up that make others adore you. Some examples of softs skill are:

- creativity/innovative thinking
- communication

---

45   "Hard Skills vs. Soft Skills," Indeed, November 25, 2020, www.indeed.com/career-advice/resumes-cover-letters/hard-skills-vs-soft-skills.

- critical thinking
- collaboration
- adaptability
- leadership
- big-picture thinking
- self-awareness
- growth mindset

Note that some of these are cultivated mindsets (critical thinking, adaptability, growth mindset, big-picture thinking), a few are based on EQ (communication, collaboration, self-awareness), and others are personal characteristics (creativity, leadership).

None of these soft skills get the job done on their own. No one is going to hire you to "be creative." They'll hire you to produce a product, and your creativity will help you deliver a new and exciting product they've never seen before. Soft skills support the hard skills by either removing challenges, maintaining the environment, or enhancing the quality of the hard skill outcomes.

Cultivating the soft skills related to mindset can raise your confidence levels and allow you to proceed with your work faster and more efficiently. Cultivating soft skills related to maintaining relationship harmony means your work will not be interrupted by emotional outbursts and office politics. Cultivating soft skills related to personal characteristics means a range of positive benefits such as producing better work unique to yourself and raising your value tremendously.

Soft skills may not get the job done, but they allow the job to get done with maximum efficiency and impact while minimizing roadblocks along the way. Now let's talk about getting the job done.

What Are Hard Skills?

You may be saying, "I hear you, but I want to get more into the real, tangible stuff. EQ is going to take time for me to get my head around."

I understand. We started this book talking about the importance of stacking hard skills and then walked through chapters of soft skills instead. But this preparation has been crucial to your ability to identify the right skill sets to cultivate. And only with soft skills can you actually leverage those hard skills once you master them.

Yes, hard skills are what actually gets your job done. When your boss says, "Crunch these numbers," you crunch them. When your coworker asks you to edit their written work, you apply your editing skill. At some point, your work success comes down to being able to actually do the job you've claimed you can do.

I suspect that you already understand hard skills, but in case you want more clarity, here are some examples:

- user experience design
- podcasting
- digital marketing
- business analysis
- sales
- product development
- public speaking
- accounting
- computer programming
- writing

If you're a market analyst, your hard skills are what allow you to analyze that market with cold, hard facts. If you are a freelance technical writer for a living (hard skill), your ability to open and close each sale (soft skill) will enable you to sustain and grow an income over time.

Customers come to you to access your hard skills. They don't have them, and they want to hire someone who does to produce something they can't create themselves. Hard skills allow you to produce what your customers are asking for. Hard skills are what you can *do*.

How to Develop Both Hard and Soft Skills

Now that you understand the difference between hard and soft skills, you're probably asking, "So . . . where do I go to learn new skills?"

You're already there. By reading this book, you've learned a whole host of new soft skills you didn't have before. Learning skills doesn't have to be a painful headache. You don't have to give up your family or go back to college. Learning new skills can really be as simple as picking up a book in your spare time and practicing what you've read. If you look closely, you'll find that skill training is all around you. You just might not have realized it before.

According to Jenny Blake, author of *Pivot*, learning isn't just pivotal to your career. It's a crucial part of your growth and overall well-being. Jenny says that if you're an impactor and you're in a role where you've stopped learning and growing, there's almost no amount of money that can keep you there. You will start to become increasingly more miserable. And boredom, studies show, can manifest in the body the same way that stress does.

How can you avoid being bored, stressed, and miserable? Seek out learning opportunities with intention. The easiest place to start is within your current company, wherever you're working right now. You may not have considered how many free resources your company offers its employees to diversify their skill sets. It's in every company's best interests to grow their workers and diversify their existing talent pool. It's likely your company also offers a wealth of skill development opportunities right at your fingertips.

Try speaking to your manager and asking about opportunities to work on cross-functional teams. Does your company offer rotations? Can you shift into a different role within the company to learn a new skill? Are there trainings offered to help educate you from within? Are there any volunteer opportunities your company puts together where you can learn new skills while networking with people and giving

151

back to the community? Does your company take part in any business resource groups, or do your executives keep memberships in groups that you could join?

Many HR departments offer free training available right on the company's intranet. Have you looked into what free training your company desperately hopes you'll take part in? Does your company partner with other companies to offer discounted training you could jump into?

Have you shared your desire to grow and advance with your management team? Have you asked for suggestions on where to learn or what skills to focus on? Have you asked them how they accomplished their own growth and who helped them advance?

Before you worry about forging into the wilds beyond your company, make sure you're taking full advantage of every resource being offered right in your own backyard. It could be that your company has been dropping hints all along and you never got the memo. Check into what you can get right now, for free or cheap, that will help enhance your usefulness to your company, demonstrate your work ethic and desire to grow, and impress those around you.

When you've exhausted those resources, or if your compass points in a direction your current employer doesn't seem to be going, then it's time to venture outside those four walls. Forge your own path. You've already figured out where your passions are and how to discover new interests. Put them to the test and study what the forerunners are doing in those new industries.

YouTube is another major resource for people looking to learn. Google certifications can give you tangible proof of a host of new hard skills to get jobs done. Coursera lets you build your skill sets online by taking classes from top institutions. LinkedIn Learning (formerly Lynda.com) has customized courses that can connect to your LinkedIn for a fully personal experience.

There are less formal approaches as well. Sites like Udemy and Gumroad allow upcoming stars to share their skill sets for next to nothing. Twenty dollars and an evening watching videos on these sites may give you the edge you need in a new industry.

Some people make their entire living teaching hard skills to others. If you find these people, verify their credentials and reputation to make sure they're worth learning from. On a rainy Saturday afternoon, you could radically transform your skill set with a whole new approach that finally brings your career mashup into reality.

Speaking of professionals building skills at a blistering pace, Mehtab Bhogal cofounded his own private equity firm, Karta Ventures, at age twenty-four. His story leaves me awestruck. He built himself up on Facebook by doing over $500,000 of business, then grabbed a partner and shifted into equity.

As a teenager, Mehtab was diagnosed with spinal stenosis and degenerative disc disease. Conventional jobs just weren't going to work for him. Now he steps into distressed companies, identifies their challenges, and rebuilds them stronger than before. Talk about a constant skill challenge!

I also know professionals who aim to pivot into more creative industries. They may be accountants by day, but on their lunch breaks they're watching YouTube tutorials on how to write fiction or build a DJ playlist. You don't have to quit your job to find the time to cultivate new skills.

Applying Hard and Soft Skills to the Business of You

As you find new skills you want to learn and seek out training that teaches them, you also have to master them. That means practice, practice, practice.

There's a saying that it takes ten thousand hours to truly master a skill. If you're not perfect at your new skills on your very first try, give yourself permission to be terrible at them. In fact, author and entrepreneur Chris Krimitsos has a fundamental philosophy of starting ugly. It's not about getting it right the first time but rather making that mindset shift, acknowledging those limitations and still starting with whatever you have. It's accepting that failure is an inevitable part of your business and career journey.

Once you've reached a point where you've made real progress and achieved success with some level of consistency, show your skills to others. Don't keep them hidden under your bed. Share your skills with the world, talk to others in your new industry, and network around with people who share that skill. Learn from them too. Keep improving.

If your new skill is really important to your personal fulfillment, then pivot in a new direction to apply that skill professionally. Maybe you can transition within your company to a new role that allows you to leverage that new skill. Or you can volunteer somewhere on the weekend to utilize what you've learned.

Gathering skills is excellent. Creating a mashup from your wealth of skills is better. Find ways to combine your new skills with your old skills to shift in surprising new directions that other people haven't thought of yet. (We'll talk about this more in the next chapter). Your mashup is the whole purpose of this book, so don't keep your skills in separate boxes. Mix them around and see what pops out.

Practice your soft skills too. Analyze how every job interview, client sales call, or customer conversation goes. When you attend events, practice reading the room and expanding your network. Networking enhances your EQ and strengthens your soft skills.

Put together an elevator pitch about yourself and update it to include your newest skill mashup. List some of your top skills and the way they interact with each other to give you a unique value no one else can match.

As the chief growth officer at design firm Essential, David Knies knows about branding. As a young man, David always wanted to play professional soccer in Europe or be James Bond, but he didn't have the skills to do either. So when he graduated, the offers weren't exactly flying his way.

But that didn't stop David.

David has since spent the last thirty years working deep inside the global innovation economy at the intersection of design, management consulting, venture capital, innovation, strategy, brand, product, marketing, and even executive recruiting.

After being in marketing leadership roles for a good portion of his career, David went through his own pivot as he realized those marketing-focused positions didn't play to his full strengths. He had to come up with his own brand strategy, figure out how he was unique, and discover how he could create value for an employer or a client. Then he had to learn how to pitch it—because it's one thing to say it, but it's another thing to actually get people to pay for it.

Having had a range of skills and experiences, David got to work branding himself as a unique entity with a range of skills no one else could match. Personal brand strategy is really understanding how to view yourself as a product and what you offer as a service, and how to best position that in the market to leverage your own unique strengths or superpowers. To David, the goal of this mashup was to pitch himself as a completely unique product that employers and customers *can't live without*.

Measuring Your Success

How do you know when you're doing this skills thing right? Measuring success on skills can seem vague. Hard skills are easier to track because you'll be delivering better work and probably making more money. But soft skills are tougher.

Let's look at three measurements for tracking successful skill growth and application.

Hard Skill Progress

The best way to measure your progress is to watch how others react to your accomplishments and work.

As your hard skills increase, others will likely treat you as a source of information and wisdom in that area. They'll seek you out for advice based on functional expertise, or they'll ask you for insights about the industry. They may ask you to speculate on what competitors are doing or how to outflank them with smarter moves. Or they might ask you to think up new directions for your skills—new mashups you've invented or could invent due to your wide range of abilities.

Pay attention to how your boss responds to you. Be the utility player that can pivot, flex, and adapt rapidly as the dynamics within your environment change. You become more valuable as a generalist that can integrate all the dots over time than the position player who remains limited by their narrow skill set. And as you show these changes, your boss should comment on it. They may give you more responsibility or even turn to you for advice and insight.

When you've become the expert, and everyone else treats you like one, you know you've mastered that hard skill.

Soft Skill (EQ) Progress

Soft skills are harder to measure, but there are a few ways to figure out if you're progressing. For example, is there less friction in your team and perhaps more harmony? Are people angry at you less often and smiling at you more? Do you notice people seem more relaxed in your presence? Are they eager to get your approval?

Are you feeling more heard and understood? Are your communications more clear and articulate? Are you getting better responses when you reach out to new people to network? Has your network grown? Have your connections with people deepened?

One useful way to test your EQ is to talk with your boss and coworkers after meetings to compare insights and see if they came out with the same takeaways. Try to find congruence with them. If they're sharing insights that blow you away, that tells you that your EQ might need some work. But by gathering insight and comparing, you're already working on it! And if the other parties are blown away by your insights, that tells you all your hard work on soft skills is paying off.

As your EQ and soft skills increase, people will come to you for advice on resolving issues that aren't purely related to getting the job done. They'll ask about how to improve a work relationship, manage a concern, or cultivate better productivity. You might be called on to mediate a misunderstanding between coworkers. Or your boss may stop in now and then to ask for your insights on how you feel the office is running and what behaviors need to be handled before they become issues.

Just like with hard skills, when people start to seek your insight, you've become an expert, an influencer, and possibly a leader. That's the best indicator of progress.

Overall Success

How do you measure your overall success?

Look closely at all of your professional relationships. People respect results. Applying your skills should get results. You should notice more harmony at work, more personal fulfillment, lower stress levels, better conversations with the people you interact with each day, and perhaps even an increase in income.

If you're making those results known, you should also be receiving recognition. I'm not suggesting you brag about your latest accomplishments to everyone within earshot of the watercooler, searching for compliments. Simply update your LinkedIn profile with your new endeavors and contribute to success at work. Not every person you meet will applaud you for your latest new skill. You're always going to have ungrateful or grumpy people who don't validate you. But the people who really matter—the experts you look up to, your boss, and your coworkers—how are they responding to you?

Deepak Shukla has a story that gives frustrated careerists hope. As the founder and CEO of the SEO agency Pearl Lemon, Deepak's career path has taken a meandering course through a truly breathtaking range of industries and jobs. He worked as a tax consultant, ran a recording studio and a tutoring company, and trained with the British Special

Forces. Twenty-three jobs—all before the age of twenty-five. Talk about a huge range of skill sets to learn.

Without specialization, Deepak could have grown frustrated. Instead he got comfortable with the change. Abnormal became normal for him. He learned to flow effortlessly through a range of roles and tasks. Eventually he founded his own SEO company and became the CEO in charge of it all. His adaptability and huge mashup of unique skills helped him build a career path no one else could ever hope to replicate, and that makes him invaluable wherever he goes.

How do you feel after making changes? Are you more satisfied than before? Are you closer to your goals? The best indicator of success is if you're moving closer to your ultimate goal and feeling good about where you're going. Your life satisfaction should be going up, not down.

Don't be afraid to ask others for feedback. Instead of guessing how others see you, ask them. Send out your latest project and see how people respond. Show your skills to your boss and ask them how your work has changed. Feedback from others is a crucial component to understanding how you're changing. After all, you're with yourself every single day. It can be hard to see changes when you're inside your own head twenty-four seven. Get feedback from others and use it to chart your progress.

And always remember that skills aren't the goal in and of themselves. They're a means to an end, not the end itself. You can collect all the skills in the world, but you won't be satisfied if you don't apply them in a meaningful way. Make sure you're not cultivating your skills in secret. Master them and use them!

Skills Assessment: Exercise

Based on your plan, you've probably already identified some core skills you should develop to achieve your goals. The networking conversations you've been having also should be giving you more insight into the types of skills you need, further refining your plan.

Let's review your plan and identify any additional hard and soft skills you need to complete it. Make a list of all missing skills you've identified so far, as well as what else to consider based on conversations you've had or on your research from early on.

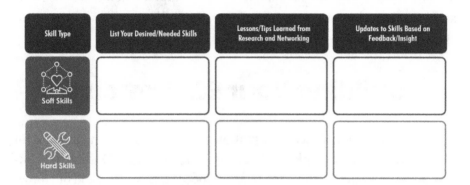

Skill Type	List Your Desired/Needed Skills	Lessons/Tips Learned from Research and Networking	Updates to Skills Based on Feedback/Insight
Soft Skills			
Hard Skills			

Example: Project Management

Let's say you want to pivot into a project management role in a new industry. Start by researching that industry to gain knowledge around what's going on. You learn that certain technologies being developed will disrupt everything. You could look at the suppliers that support the development of that tech and assess, *What do they want? What do they need?* Maybe they're great at development and coding but need project managers to help accelerate the launch of the technology into the marketplace. Or perhaps they need an agile expert in a specific area. You can find where they have gaps and position yourself to fulfill that need.

Go look at their LinkedIn job postings and identify some of their requirements. Maybe that company has their needs on full blast and is desperately looking for a project manager to solve their notorious issues. And don't panic if you don't fulfill every certification requirement. These certifications are the next skills you'll master. There are multiple ways to get certifications online. Scrum Master is a really good option for this, as is Udemy, Coursera, and edX.

Then get to work on the skills and certifications you need to fulfill that new role. Think of these skill development sessions as "sprints." You have a hard focus on learning a particular skill with the goal of being able to say, "Yes, I can do that for you. I'm in the process of earning my certification for this. It will be complete on this date." Show self-generated initiative, and employers and clients alike will want to snatch you up before a competitor does.

Building Your EQ: Exercise

Think about the most recent virtual or in-person meeting you had with a coworker, boss, or employee (a one-on-one meeting). Outline the context of the situation—define the purpose, people, activities, and outcome.

Now let's dive deeper into the dynamics and subsequently break down the meeting. Consider the situation from *your* vantage point and ask yourself the following perspective questions:

- How did I feel?
- How did I react/behave?
- What did I do or say?
- How did I do or say it?

Now look at the situation from the perspective of the other person involved and ask yourself the following perspective questions:

- What are they dealing with in their job and personal life?
- How do I think they feel?
- How did they react/behave?
- What did they do or say?
- How did they do or say it?

Where are the gaps between how you perceived and reacted to the meeting and how the other person did? What would you do differently now that you know where potential disconnects are? How could that have changed the outcome?

You can then steer the outcome of your next meeting. **It's not just about what you said, it's making sure you each understand what the other person said and why.**

EQ Skill-Building Tips

Going forward, record your conversations when possible and then review them. This is how you can train yourself to "read the room" better by observing others' behaviors and yours. It also helps you understand what you could have done better or differently in that situation.

Reconnect with the other people after the meeting to ensure you understood what they said. This means following up with them and paraphrasing what you've heard so far, or asking them to paraphrase what they've heard. It closes the cognitive gap and shows that you care.

If you need more personal interaction to practice building your EQ, apply for jobs and go on interviews. You don't have to intend to take the new job. Knowing that you're wanted can give you a shot of confidence, and it gives you a great way to get used to high-pressure social situations where you need to deliver your elevator pitch to an expectant audience. And who knows? Maybe during this practice you'll actually discover the next job of your dreams.

Remember that it's important to take inventory of other people's feelings and behaviors, because relationships are a two-way street. You can't build EQ until you understand the dynamics from all sides, and that means getting feedback from others.

It may seem tough at first. You have to do this in real time as well as review what happened retroactively. That can intimidate people. But no one says you have to do it fast. Slowing down your interactions can sometimes help cultivate better EQ and give you time to think. It's perfectly OK to ask the other person for a moment to think, as this shows you're taking the conversation seriously. Go at your own pace, breathe, and don't panic.

Building Your Hard Skills: Exercise

Pick a hard skill you want to master that will have the most impact on getting you to where you want to go. Break down that skill into smaller, more manageable parts and put it in a realistic time frame. Start to execute those smaller tasks to establish proficiency of that skill.

The exercise below enables you to acquire all the hard skills you'll need to fluidly navigate the new world of work for the rest of your career—and life.

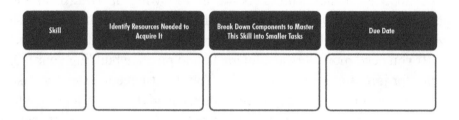

Skill	Identify Resources Needed to Acquire It	Break Down Components to Master This Skill into Smaller Tasks	Due Date

By this point in the book, you've got a handle on both the hard and soft skills you have—and the ones you know you must have. You also understand how (and why) to enhance your emotional intelligence.

Everything we've covered in this chapter and in the previous steps of this road map apply to you as an individual, but they also apply to the organizations you work for, run, or even found. In the next chapter, we're going to recontextualize the road map to building the business of you to work within a company. That way *everyone* can navigate the new world of work successfully.

CHAPTER 8

The Fluid Organization

By this point in the journey, you're well on your way to fluidity mastery and self-empowerment maximization. You already know how to craft yourself into the ultimate worker for the new world of work. And that's wonderful. The title of the book, after all, is *Building the Business of You*.

Except, if you've been paying attention, you've seen me tell you that your productivity, skills, and impact travel far beyond yourself. You know you need other successful and hardworking people to help you grow into your true self.

If you're reading this book, there's a good chance you're in a leadership position, or you see yourself in one someday soon. People with the ambition to study and refine themselves tend to rise, because they're willing to put in the work. They're valuable to organizations. *You* are valuable.

The good news is that everything in this book becomes even more relevant to leadership roles. You can take any chapter in this book and apply it to your organization. Just as the individual must learn to navigate this new world of work, so must companies. The new rules apply all the way up and down the chain. And by building your organization into a dynamic one, a more fluid system, you provide a shelter for individual workers in this turbulent work era.

A fluid company can adapt and thrive in an uncertain and ever-changing world. A fluid company has the ability to quickly pivot and capitalize on opportunities better than competitors. A fluid company can harness the expansive skill sets and passions of its employees to catapult them to the next level. By helping your employees build their own compasses in addition to establishing that strategic plan for your organization, you'll be able to align needs, interests, passions, and purpose to unleash everyone's potential.

Keep in mind that you are not the sole focal point of your business. You need to take a wide-angle view. Understand the value of everybody that works for you. Embrace their professional and personal dreams the same way you do your own. If you make yourself the only important person in the organization, your best workers will leave. Leadership is about being the coach and not necessarily the star player.

Great leaders have empathy. They listen. And they work hard to set a course for the future and provide a positive example to their team. To that end, train your teams to listen. Employee development doesn't only take place through direct mentoring. Your people need to understand that growth also happens through listening and observing, which are both critical ways to learn. Yes, showing your team how to accomplish their tasks matters. But listening and observing as they develop and embracing their needs are also crucial elements of leadership.

Maybe you're reading this book because you're already in a position to influence hiring, training, and management of workers. You're here because you want to learn to build a dynamic system to survive the market. I'll show you how to do that.

Other readers aren't necessarily looking to shake up their entire organization. Maybe you have group workers who aren't a cultural or skill-set fit. So far, managing them has felt like herding cats. By the end of this chapter, you should know how to approach them in a more productive manner than ever before.

So what does it mean to be a leader and apply the principles taught in this book? Let's take a look first at how each of the five main points of this book apply to your organization. After that, I've got a whole host of hiring strategies you need to build the ultimate fluid team.

Spotting the Trends (Internally and Externally)

Remember way back at the beginning of the book when we talked about analyzing both the market and yourself? I taught you how to stay on top of market trends, spot opportunities, and position yourself as the expert in your industry. You also learned to take a ruthless and objective assessment of your own strengths and gaps with the goal of fixing them.

All of these tactics are doubly important when you run an organization. You as an individual may be able to adapt to market changes on short notice. But unless you are a fast-moving start-up or a scale-up company, it's likely that your organization operates more like a large ship: it takes a while to turn that heavy bulk. Failure to identify trends means you'll fall behind your competition. What employee wants to work in a company five years behind the times that produces products already way out of season?

And just as important as it is to identify your own strengths and gaps, an organization requires as much thought and assessment. You can't run an efficient team with glaring weaknesses and problems you ignore. Your team will underperform, spend half their time battling for power, or leave you behind and give you a nasty reputation in the business world. You also won't unlock your greatest potential as an organization if you don't leverage your best strengths to their fullest.

So let's talk about spotting the trends and what to do with them.

Externally

Here's where you study to understand the market, your target audience, and your competition. The external trends help you to build that business strategy.

The good news is that this becomes so much simpler in an organization. You can actually hire someone to do all the detailed research and analysis for you. This may be an independent contractor you bring on. Or maybe you designate someone within your organization who loves research and recalibrate their job description to include this type of work. If they already love staying on top of trends, embrace that. If they excel at and truly enjoy data collection and analysis, help take their skills to the next level by having them study competitors' sales numbers and seasonal earnings reports.

Notice that I'm encouraging you to find someone who loves this sort of work. Remember how I told you to identify and embrace your own passions? As the boss, you get to help other people do the same. A happy worker is a productive worker, and giving someone a chance to pivot into this role could earn you a loyal employee for many years to come. Be the boss who gives people a chance to embrace their passions.

Spotting the trends is also a job you are likely doing yourself given your role as a leader—or at least you should definitely start to. You need to constantly identify what's on the horizon and determine the "so what" and "now what" answers you need to thrive. Being able to see around the corner enables you to capitalize on opportunities, manage risk and expectations, and even dynamically pivot to ensure you can create or build on the traction you have.

Internally

But to really match your workers up with the best roles for them, you're going to have to spot the trends inside your own organization. That means looking at strengths, gaps, and challenges. You need to understand what you do well (and not so well) as a team, what really differentiates your group from others, and the true value you bring.

Analyzing your team's strengths may look like sitting down with each individual on staff and interviewing them again, just like you should have during the hiring process. Get to know them in a less formal way by asking them what sort of work excites them and see how that has meshed with their work performance against that work if you can. Even prod with questions until you uncover some interests and hobbies.

You may have a young worker and you're their first employer, so they've got no experience thinking about what sort of work they enjoy. But maybe they've got a hobby that translates into a work skill, like playing chess or reading nonfiction. Perfect! The chess player may thrive in a strategy-oriented position. The nonfiction reader may be the market analyst of your dreams.

Take notes and build a for-your-eyes-only file on each member of staff, including yourself. Write down what everyone is especially good at and where their passions intersect with work skills. You're documenting skill sets and the potential to develop exciting new skills to meet organizational needs you may not know you have. When a new problem arises six months from now, you can consult your list and pivot your best person into a new role to handle it.

By matching up your employees with their passions and favorite sort of work, you'll become that awesome boss who can unleash the full potential of their people. And that reputation carries immense weight when it comes time to hire new employees that bring in a fresh set of skills.

Also look at the way your team works together. Individuals have strong points, but so do organizations. And don't just focus on the hard skills but also what it takes to create a strong culture.

Maybe your team maintains perfect harmony and cohesion, with zero office infighting. That may not seem like it sells you more products or earns money, but you cannot put a price on that level of peaceful efficiency. Try running a sales office where everyone hates each other and you'll see how valuable this strength is.

When you identify those gaps, look at where your organization needs to fill the holes. Maybe you design the best T-shirts and pants in the industry, but you've got no idea how to expand your product line. You need an expert on accessorizing with your main product to increase sales numbers in new markets.

Or maybe your company blew up faster than you expected, and now you're struggling to keep it together. Do you need to bring in a vice president? Or even two, to each handle half the company? How do you scale with the right people and resources that can take you where you want to go?

Look at your operational side. Are they run ragged with minimal staff? You might outsource your IT needs instead of making your operations manager handle them on top of their other duties. Or maybe they just need an assistant to help balance their load.

Look at where you're underperforming, falling behind the market, or just not driving objectives the way you'd like. Map those team strengths onto the gaps and see if someone could pivot into a new role. If not, hire a new employee or an outside contractor to handle it for you.

As a leader, you must survey the dynamics of your team and those around you. Who's struggling, who's thriving, who's challenging, and why? You must do that gap analysis and determine how to bridge the divides. It comes back to spotting those strengths, challenges, near-term opportunities, and longer-term potential. How can you connect the dots for those on your team? Or even for those who aren't, but with whom you work closely, to help them along the way?

Spotting the trends also means watching how your employees interact with one another and how your system runs throughout the day, week, month, and year. Look for genuine problem areas. If your employees are utterly exhausted halfway through the winter season, figure out a way to boost their morale. Maybe you've got someone in your organization who loves to plan parties and would adore a chance to throw a company New Year's celebration to encourage everyone during the winter blues.

Understand what motivates those on your team. How does what they do fit into their life goals? It's about getting to know them as people too. Remember, the human element is so crucial these days. People want to really connect with others. And as a leader, your empathy and ability to relate to your team will set you apart.

Do 360-degree reviews for your employees so you can identify areas of strength that they wouldn't have recognized themselves. Conversely, this can also highlight blind spots that team members need to address that are inhibiting them in their work and relationships.

And when you analyze genuine problems, be just as ruthless. The last thing you need is a toxic worker who drives employees to want to leave your team. That's not just a gap, that's a serious liability to your organization. Sometimes a person is just a bad fit, or an entire section of the company has become poisoned with serious negativity from a bad worker you hired. Own your role and put an end to the issue. A bad employee doesn't just cost you five or even six figures a year. That's hundreds of thousands of dollars you're flushing away in decreased productivity, bad company reputation, and destroyed morale.

An easy way to keep a handle on internal trends is to cultivate an open-door policy with your workers. Make sure they know they can come to you with concerns, ideas, and dreams. Don't put the entire process on your own shoulders. Utilize your dynamic team of smart individuals to keep their eyes on the inside and outside business happening in your company.

And make sure you're analyzing your organization the same way you analyze yourself.

Realize that everyone on your team can be a source to spot the trends, internally and externally, based on what they do. They are constantly interacting with each other and have a unique point of view of what's going on in your organization and in the wider industry. Tap into that source of knowledge. Learn to channel all those perspectives into powerful insights to help you build your strategic plan. This wider feedback is essential for your organization's compass. Employees want to have involvement in shaping the direction of their team, organization, or company. Giving them opportunities to contribute and unleash skills and capabilities that they didn't even know they had to scan the future, see the white spaces, and map out implications and recommendations drives them to engage in a different way.

Kim Scott gives excellent advice on identifying your team's dynamics in her book *Radical Candor: Be a Kick-Ass Boss without Losing Your Humanity*. She describes her own process of learning that not every professional is motivated to push into the next big thing. Pushing too hard, she says, may motivate the people looking to jump ahead in their career, but it risks alienating the people who are perfectly happy with the job they're doing. She separates these two groups into Superstars and Rockstars.

Rockstars, she says, love their work. They've found their rhythm, so to speak. They see no reason to change jobs. They're the rocks of a company—steady, dependable, reliable. They'll stick with you so long as you nurture them and keep them happy.

Superstars charge ahead and want to make visible gains. They need to be constantly challenged and given new opportunities. Their mentality is all about growth, and if you want to keep them around, you need to show them how you're providing the best opportunity to grow.

The real takeaway is that you have to be engaged and in tune with your workforce just as much as you expect them to be engaged with your organization. Remember this is the part where you are gathering the needed intel to help you see the bigger picture and discern those subsequent implications to get ahead. Spotting the internal trends helps you cultivate the best teams to accomplish your collective goals.

Creating Your Compass

How can a company run without clarity on where they want to go and what they stand for? Acquiring new customers and getting existing ones to buy more from you may seem like good enough business goals for the first six months, but to really sustain as an organization you're going to need a compass.

What is your company's mission and vision? What are their goals and objectives, and how do they align to yours? Where does your compass point? If you have no idea, where on earth are you leading people?

You built your individual compass by figuring out your vision and a pathway to get there. Do the same with your organization. What strategies and tactics does your team need to employ to move the business forward in a measurable way? How do the company principles and values (as well as ones you personally hold) permeate into what you and your team need to do every day?

It's all about working to build strategic plans for your organization and for the people within it. That all can occur with a clear plan in place. You'll also attract customers who value those same principles, so identify who you'd rather work with and include that as part of your company compass.

Scott DiGiammarino is the CEO of MovieComm and a master at building unified teams around mutual goals. He says that creating an engaged workforce requires buy-in based on a clear vision as well as shared principles and values. But it also takes ongoing communication and measurement around the heartbeat of the organization to set things in motion and sustain momentum. You as the leader need to figure out how to make those principles come alive for your team as well as translating the overarching business goals and objectives of your company into something that is tangible and relatable to your employees.

To be an effective leader, one who matters and is relevant, you have to create a clear and compelling vision that gets everyone aligned and committed. As Scott says, "If they don't understand why they're doing what they're doing, there's no reason in the world why they're going to give their best efforts." This is why creating your compass (or really compasses) matters. Building that plan to get everyone on the same page is so critical to ensure that all folks are moving in the same direction toward the same goals. That creates traction and momentum instead of friction and inertia. You are creating alignment between everyone in your organization, from strategy through execution.

Leaders seek out Leadership Strategies founder Michael Wilkinson when they need guidance on how to build a thriving organization. Michael views alignment as a funnel or flowchart where each level depends on the one below it. You have vision, then objectives or measures of success, then critical success factors—the strategies and tactics for getting you there. When there is an issue with alignment, it's because one of these is off. Thus, misalignment issues come down to conflicting visions of an outcome or an inability to effectively communicate between the various parties. A clear organizational compass prevents this. From strategy through execution you are working to ensure that you get this solid flow. If everyone is clear on what their tasks are based on agreed upon strategies, you're more likely to hit the goals and objectives you set.

Realize that your guiding principles and values, your goals and objectives, are not limited to being only financial in nature. Delivering on that higher-order purpose—being that business for good—also matters, because your employees are not solely focused on money. So once your financial goals are addressed, ask yourself what else you (and your employees) would like your organization to accomplish. Figure out what additional goals your company holds apart from pure profit. Add those factors into your compass as well.

Maybe you'd like to reinvest a portion of that money into your local community and build your city from poverty to prosperity. It could be that you'd like to mentor new prodigies and be known as the best company for talented young workers to build their first professional victories. Or maybe your clothing company decides to create an entire division geared toward helping clothe the less fortunate.

Gather feedback from your staff. Imagine sending out a questionnaire asking your employees to help shape the cultural footprint of the company they work for. That creates some serious buy-in, some personal investment in the future of the company. It also tells your workers their input is valued and that they have agency in shaping the organization's vision.

Now you've built a compass to guide your company during every decision. This compass will sustain your organization during the long years ahead.

In the same way, you can help your employees develop their own compasses. Taking on younger workers fresh out of school or at the start of their career path means you can help shape them into engines of purpose. Instead of leaving them to drift for ten years and figure out their paths on their own, you can guide them to cultivating their own goals and objectives.

Talking about compasses will also weed out any workers who are just there for the profit. They're likely going to jump ship the moment a bigger payout comes along, anyway. And if introducing values and goals beyond the money drives them away, that means they weren't a good fit.

This compass also helps you give workers the best growth assistance. When individuals on your team have clarity on where they want to go, you can help them reach their potential. Everyone in your organization, regardless of where they are in their career, needs a compass—they need to know what they are working toward. And remember: it's always more than just title and money. For some it may be clear; others need help on how to shape it and want to create their own mashups. They want to know what their path is within your organization and need help finding it. As a leader, guide them in building their plan to help them see the bigger picture with timing and metrics to create forward movement.

By aligning both company and individual compasses, you can ensure everyone is on the same page and working toward similar goals for your organization. And these compass questions are a great way to conduct useful interviews to determine the best fit for your hiring needs.

Preparing for Change

In Chapter 5, Preparing for Change, we talked about managing your individual fears about performance, expectations, and outcomes so you can be fluid and adapt to constant change. When it comes to organizations, you need to manage both your own fears about being a boss and your employees' and coworkers' fears about instability, as well as their individual fears just like your own.

Let's start with you. Are you comfortable being the boss? Being the one taking risks? If you're not at the top of the company, are you comfortable with the responsibility you've been handed? Are you terrified to stick your neck out and give suggestions on how to improve the system? Are you worried you'll hire the wrong person?

Beat catastrophizing by grounding yourself in reality. Manage the expectations others have of you without letting them hold you back. Recognize that fear of growth guarantees your organization will stagnate under your watch. And stagnation is death. Better to grow, even just a little bit, than to stay the same and die.

The chief people officer at Frontpoint Security, Bhavna Dave, encourages professionals to speak up and act in the best interests of their organization and themselves. "Don't let your job description define what your impact can be. It's OK to swim outside your lane sometimes if you think that's the right thing to do for the organization, and make sure you're bringing people along with you. Don't let the job description define your impact."

Push past any level of discomfort to voice your opinion and perspective. You may have valuable insight your company needs to adjust and thrive. And speaking up with potential solutions or new approaches is a great way to get noticed. Valuable CEOs will embrace ideas from all angles, and they'll want to keep you around if you're providing helpful insight.

And when it comes to fears of hiring the wrong people, don't worry: at some point, you will hire the wrong person—it happens. At some time or another, you'll hire a worker who completely underperforms—they can't do the job well at all. Maybe they'll slip through your hiring process and unpleasantly surprise you by lacking all the skills they claimed they had. Or they'll seem charming at the interview and turn out to be completely toxic once inside. Or maybe they'll be a genuinely good person who experiences a sudden life crisis that changes who they are for the worse.

It's not about getting it perfect or never making mistakes. You're spotting the trends and staying on top of things, both internally and externally. And as an organization, it doesn't fall completely on your shoulders to spot problems anymore. If you hire the wrong person, you'll hear about it from your team. Trust me, it's immediately clear when a piece doesn't fit in the jigsaw puzzle. The key isn't to be perfect but to respond in the best possible way that sets you up for greater success in the future.

Manage your employees' fears the same way. Address their concerns about changes with frank communication. When organizations plan big changes, they tend to fall back on company memos full of buzzwords and marketing gibberish. Workers spot these from a mile away and get more frustrated. Instead, address employee fears directly and honestly. Acknowledge the concerns. Agree that change is scary. Transparency is key.

Then manage expectations. Commit to making the change together. It's about showing you care on a personal level and want to help. You are building trust, and that happens through clear communications. Share some of the fluidity exercises from this book and teach them where you're going. Get your workers on board with your goals by sharing those goals openly. Remember the company compass you just created? That's a fantastic way to tell your workers where you're all headed now.

A team with a clear mission and a trusted leader is a team that gets the job done. This is about ensuring you help prepare your staff for the impending changes that will always be occurring in your organization. Change is incredibly uncomfortable, and many don't want to fail, particularly in this uncertain environment. Identify the root cause of their fear, stress, or anxiety (and make sure to help them understand the root as well) so they can push through what is holding them back. Guide them to realize what are realistic outcomes versus those they may be projecting.

Your team may struggle with fear of the unknown or be anxious about some aspect of the project they are working on. Help them become aware of their stress and help them work through it. The point is not for you to shoulder their burden or take on their stress yourself. Instead, work together to solve the problem like you would any other work challenge. That could look like giving them enough information about your business plan so that they feel like the future is not unknown and terrifying but well planned and achievable.

For Jennifer Trzepacz, COO and partner at Wildcat Venture Partners, communication is king in team building. Most teams dive into the "what," Jennifer says. It's, "Let's get this done," without, "Here's how." They may talk about the how as it relates to tech: "Oh, we'll use this software, we'll use this application," but they don't talk about the "how" for each other. How does the application affect their working relationship every day?

In other words, if you don't share your plan with your team, they have no idea where they're supposed to aim. They'll suspect you don't know either. And you honestly may not know. Communicating with your team forces you to define your own plans in concrete terms. It slows you down and makes you lay out the step-by-step guide for what's going to happen. And that's invaluable for both you and your team.

It also addresses any confusion or lack of clarity around what they have to do, which in turn alleviates fears and insecurities that may have been brewing. As Jennifer said, "There is no replacement for that one-on-one exchange that you need to have at some point in time in building trust in that relationship." You want your team to trust you? Talk to them.

Helping others manage their fears isn't limited to just your direct employees or team members. With the world of work being such a highly collaborative system, you will have peers that may also be struggling with sudden changes that impact their role and organization. So building a rhythm when you work with them is critical to finding common ground to move efforts forward.

The keyword in all of this is trust. Helping alleviate and manage fears involves building a trusted relationship with those on your team with whom you work. You have to know and care about them to spot the trends creating the angst that leads to the fear to begin with. You could do that by going out to lunch or coffee in a setting outside of work. Get to know them personally and help to decipher what could be really going on. It's about you connecting the dots for them.

It's about taking a proactive approach, and communication is essential. Keep this in mind if they seem closed off at first. Fear can make us withdraw in anticipation of pain. It may involve more work on your part to ask questions and extract clarity from them. But persist. And keep communicating.

Recognize that you can't solve every anxiety. It may be that some of your workers need professional help managing their mental health. Making sure your workers have access to these resources in advance means you can support them as human beings and get them back on track to productivity faster than workers left to suffer without help.

It's important to not forget that a business needs to be as human as it can possibly be because your success comes down to your people. It has to be authentic and true in the small moments and big ones. Great leaders genuinely care about the people they lead—and they show it. Talk to your workers about how they are doing and work to identify the underlying drivers of behavior, from compensation to praise to the mood in the office or their home office setup. Once you know their concerns, work together to come up with a solution to manage them.

An example scenario: Imagine people on your current team have to take on different roles because of some strategic decisions in the company. There's a new initiative that will help pivot the company in a new direction. It has significant exposure and opportunity for incredible growth. But it's pressure filled, and all eyes will be on it. Folks are uncomfortable because they haven't performed these roles before and they fear failing.

The solution: Talk to your team members to determine where they have the most fear and anxiety. Play out those worrying scenarios to help them see what's real and what isn't. Build a plan to tackle areas where they can start to build momentum and confidence in their new roles. Follow up with frequent one-on-one meetings to check in and see what progress they have made and continually work on what holds them back to give them increased confidence.

Managing all these fears will help prepare your organization for greater fluidity. Providing the best possible support system for your employees serves as motivation and encouragement, and it helps them feel more secure with pushing out of their comfort zones and challenging themselves. Once you and your workers are free from irrational concerns and fettering expectations, you're ready to grow in exciting new directions.

Networking Your Way to Your Path

Networking is all about building your village to help you move your current and future potential initiatives forward for your company. Networking as an organization takes place both internally and externally. Let's look first at how to network outside your company.

Externally

Building relationships outside of your company is crucial in today's world. Work gets done by leveraging various vendors, service providers, agencies, consultancies, and contractors.

You will naturally build some of these external relationships as you search for those who augment your skill set. But also realize that while you may never hire someone, you will still both be able to get mutual value by exchanging thought leadership and knowledge in your respective areas. These may lead to natural partnerships in the future that help you both capitalize on opportunities due to the changing market, competition, and consumer dynamics. You can even start with the vendors you work with and ask them to connect you with others who could be beneficial to know or who can expand your knowledge in an area in which you need to build expertise.

Just like in the exercises you did for yourself, you can leverage your close personal or professional network to create introductions to others who would align with your company's needs. You may want to reach out to thought leaders in a particular space. You could leverage LinkedIn to establish that initial connection.

Having these conversations and building these relationships honestly looks much the same as what you're already doing as an individual, just on a different scale. Either you or a designated expert at your company should make sure you're connecting with both individuals and entire companies in your industry that can provide value to your organization. The same principles apply: building loose connections, determining how you can help them, and following up. And remember that networking is about connecting with them on a deeper level, not coming across as just wanting to pump them for information. All the practices you learned in the previous chapter hold true for an organization.

Internally

Internal networking is about mapping out the relationships inside your organization to help you develop, influence, support, and implement your ideas and initiatives. You won't be able to get anything done without the collective support of others in the company, so building those relationships is essential. These relationships will be cross-functional and include different levels within your organization, including between teams.

So how do you decide where to foster connections? Understand the ecosystem by which things get done and how decisions get made for your team's initiatives. Based on that, determine whom the influencers and decision makers are. Realize that an org chart doesn't always reflect who has the most impact. Then work to establish relationships with those key folks.

Start with those with whom you already have first-degree connections. Those connections could be strong ties, loose ties, or even dormant ones. As you continue to build those relationships, they will help lead you to others that are important to know. Remember that this can't be done only via email and Slack. You have to invest in getting to know them as they do you. And it's still about delivering value to the other person. You still need to plan, get to know them on a personal level, and determine how you can help them. You are working toward building a network of advocates.

You should also be helping your team create their own important connections to do their job as well. They, too, need their advocates and support systems to get them through. As a leader, your perspective is crucial to their success. You have a line of sight that they don't. And consider that they might be intimidated by reaching out to others.

For new team members who are just starting in your group, there is a lot for them to learn and likely a lot of people they need to get to know to do their job well. Help get them up to speed by mapping out their important network of relationships. Have them meet one-on-one with these folks so they can start to build rapport and trust. Your objective is to help them understand other workers' roles, their value, and how they are connected to what your employees do. It's about understanding this connective tissue that exists among people.

Helping existing employees takes much the same approach. Once you understand your ecosystem—how decisions get made, how work flows, and who your influencers are—have your employee schedule some one-on-one time with these people to build a relationship and share how they want to support their organization. It's all about deepening those internal connections.

Partner different individuals on shared projects so they have to get to know each other. Shuffle people around to both diversify their skills and grow new personal connections between workers. Have separate offices hold Zoom meetings with group activities or games. Yes, you can even schedule game time as team-building time. You'd become the most popular boss in the world. And don't forget there are entire companies you can hire to come in and build your team into a more unified work system.

Networking inside and outside your company builds new and deeper relationships that will pay dividends when it comes time to pivot and grow.

Building the Soft Skills (Not Just the Hard Skills)

As a leader, soft skills are crucial for working effectively in your role, and they are the underpinnings of great leadership. You have to excel at these to be a leader who people want to emulate and follow.

Technical/hard skills may show what you can do in your organization, but it's people skills that create opportunities for you and your team to truly advance and get things done more effectively and more efficiently. Soft skills break down barriers and open new doors.

For your team, the soft skills not only include typical ones like communication, collaboration, and problem-solving but also cultivating qualities like a growth mindset. Businesses are dynamic and constantly need to adapt, so employees need soft skills to adapt just as fast. And with work happening in teams and now virtually, you have to help others build relationships effectively and work together efficiently. That only happens with soft skills and strong EQ.

Fostering soft skills in the workplace might look like valuing a culture of idea sharing, creativity, openness, and personal leadership. Teaching employees soft skills is a fantastic way to build them into incredibly valuable employees. And while teaching someone a hard skill makes them better at leaving you for a competitor or able to start their own company, teaching the soft skills cultivates gratitude and deeper relationships at the same time, making it more likely your investment will pay off in the long term.

Yes, you should definitely provide resources and encourage your employees to gain better hard skills. You want your marketers at the top of their game and your developers creating compelling products faster and better. You need to provide these tools so they aren't spending exorbitant amounts of time on their weekends and after work trying to figure out how to get better at their jobs.

But you should also cultivate soft skills that sustain and support your organization in the long run. You do this by modeling them yourself, valuing them as a company, and bringing in speakers or providing resources to teach your employees.

Model the soft skills yourself so your employees see you exhibiting them. You might even take some time to explain what you're doing and why. Showing has the benefit of making you that boss who walks the walk. You're leading by example. That sets the tone for the entire organization.

Valuing the soft skills as a company and building a culture around them means that even resistant employees will have to learn and utilize them. Praising employees who exhibit soft skills instead of only reward-ing the hard skills is an easy way to shape worker behavior.

Cultivating the soft skills is everything to Kim Scott. According to Kim: "Your job as a leader is really to paint a picture of what's possible. And praise is a much more important tool than criticism for painting a picture of what's possible."

Reward the behaviors you want to see repeated. Eventually your team will catch on and change their behaviors to suit the new expectations.

And there are a million speakers eager to deliver a presentation at your company about the soft skills they've mastered. Maybe you pull in a therapist to talk about managing anxiety as a team. Or you hire a communications expert to teach your team better communication. That cuts down on misunderstandings and improves networking skills at the same time.

In fact, Kareen Walsh, author, CEO, and founder of the business growth strategy and executive coaching firm Revampologist, shares that the two biggest blockers in achievement within an organization are fear and misunderstanding—it's these dynamics that affect people and can prevent them from doing their best, rather than the technology or processes.

What you model, reward, and teach are what get implemented. If you want your team to value soft skills, then you and your leadership need to value them in the first place. Do that, and everything will shift into order.

Cultivating better skills in employees and leading them to greater heights is Beth Freedman's specialty. She's the CEO of dentsu X, a leading agency network. "Management is not about what you can do," Beth says, "it's about what you can get others to do, what you can teach them." She simplified it even more: "You can only do great work with great people."

If you want to do great things, invest in your people.

A Whole New Approach to People Operations

Let's talk about hiring practices. We know that people are the engines of growth, but how can you ensure you have the right ones from the start? I'll go out on a limb and say that most traditional hiring practices are counterproductive. They're haphazard, they're uninformed, and they rarely align with a company's stated mission.

What's the standard procedure to hire someone? You identify a need. You draft up a list of required credentials, experiences, and certifications you think someone who could fill that role should possess. And it could be extremely extensive because, frankly, you need someone who can do a lot of things. You put together a checklist of hard skills first. You also identify some of the cultural values or soft skills that you know will be important for a potential candidate to fit into your work environment. Then you slap that checklist up where you hope someone qualified will find it, on LinkedIn or some other website, send it to your HR contact to manage, or hire a headhunter to poach workers from other companies.

The applicant arrives in your office, online or in person. You look over their checklist of hard skills. Maybe you ask them a few questions to make sure they aren't faking their résumé. You decide you have a vaguely good feeling about them, so you pass them on to the next interviewer, who also likes them. You both shrug and decide they're probably fine to take a gamble on. And you work through this process as quickly as possible because you're desperate to get someone to fill the seat.

As you're reading this, are you realizing how limited such a process is? You're defining and assessing narrowly by default—hard skills and credentials first versus whole skills and potential. But is that really the best practice?

No. Absolutely not. We have to fix this. The truth is that job postings are a mishmash of over-the-top requirements that no human being could fulfill. Hiring teams are looking for the perfect unicorn who fits every requirement on the checklist.

Instead of hiring based on a checklist of hard skills and some soft skills, fluid organizations need to hire for aptitude. How fast can candidates adapt to the unexpected? Can they learn fast and then apply that new knowledge? Do they ask for help or struggle through and get frustrated until it's too late?

You can train someone to develop hard skills, but how can you really assess a person's soft skills or ability to learn them? How do they handle new situations? Can they adapt? Do they communicate clearly and confidently?

When you interview, bring your company mission and compass into the conversation. How do they feel about the company's core values? What do they even mean to them? How have they handled certain situations? Consider asking what they bring to the table besides your job checklist only.

You might ask, "What else do you feel you can offer this company besides helping us meet our business objectives?" If they look confused and ask, "What else is there?" then it should be a hard pass. But if they rattle off a list of soft skills? Bingo. You've found someone who understands the value of soft skills and company culture.

The idea is to try to quickly evaluate that person in a real scenario to see if, culturally, they're a good fit. If they're not, they can decide to cut ties quickly versus letting this potentially drag on. You don't know what will work and what won't work until they try.

There are different ways to assess whether the talent you are seeking will fit with your culture that doesn't involve the traditional interview process. In fact, it may not be practical or efficient to go through multiple rounds of interviews. Trying out potential talent may be the best approach, but make sure to cut ties quickly if it doesn't work out.

Crate Media has organically developed a system for figuring out if someone's a good fit for their culture. They help produce my podcast *Strategic Momentum*, and they have grown their fully remote team over the past few years. When they interview a new candidate, they ask one major question: "Are you a *Star Wars* fan?" From that answer they're able to figure out if someone shares their unique company values.

Now that's definitely a unique culture with a specific niche. But what questions like that can you ask your applicants? What values can you press them on? What indicators would make them a best fit for your culture?

Culture matters in any business. Fit is very important when creating a team that will grow the business together. And the way you may realize that is through testing and learning what characteristics work and what ones won't.

Finding the right employees is crucial, according to Lee Sommers, owner of Purpose Personal Fitness, who's worked with athletes of all levels, including Olympic champion Katie Ledecky. "A company's first focus should always be on their employees, on the people delivering the experience, because those people are the frontline of giving the experience to your customers."

Consider that for a moment. The people you hire may be the face of your organization to whoever interacts with them. Are you confident you can trust them to represent you to your various business partners? Even if they're just in billing, they're the face your customers will see when it's time to pay the bills. Make sure you're hiring a reliable representative of your corporate culture.

And are interviews really the best measurement of what someone can do? It's easy for folks to "sell" what they can do or have done. But what's a better way to assess if what they do, how they do it, and their interaction style with others creates a multiplier effect that you want instead of the productivity drain that you fear?

There's also the frequent problem of struggling to define the employee's role from the beginning. Many times there are some core skills you are looking for in a role that you want to fill, but having a utility player who can continuously learn quickly and has the aptitude and attitude to take on new challenges is of value. But with the way hiring works today, it often becomes a "check-the-box" exercise and oftentimes ends up being a situation where you are trying to hire a unicorn that doesn't exist.

True assessment of a worker's fit only really happens once they are in the company and embedded for good or for worse. So how can you evaluate for potential, performance, and cultural fit during the hiring process?

I had a conversation with Mehtab Bhogal and picked his brain about hiring. He doesn't trust the traditional interview process. He's developed his own method for choosing candidates: start small, test and learn..

"I've just found the interview, typically, it's not a great indicator of how someone will fit in culturally, so we try to structure things for that," Mehtab told me. "If they have to go, they can go quickly—or vice versa, to where if we want them more involved, we can get them more involved very fast."

Mehtab encourages leaders to use the test-and-learn approach to hiring. That is, test your applicants with real-life problems and see how fast they learn. What do they do with new information? Do they jump right into the business and apply their hard and soft skills? There's really no way to see how someone will work with your culture until they get that raw experience.

Consider giving candidates a problem to solve, setting them a task you've dealt with in the past. Maybe you even give them a challenge that's been causing you a headache. Watch how they solve it. You'll see the way their mind works, how eager they are to get the job, and what their work ethic is like. Someone can fake an interview, but they can't fake genuine work and creative problem-solving.

Perhaps you can have applicants do a case study on the market. Maybe you need a better analyst anyway. Get them to look at the market and give you a report on opportunities they see for your company to grow. This will give you valuable data on how workers outside your company see you. It also gives you insight into the skills this applicant possesses.

You could even probe their passions and soft skills and tailor the hiring experience to those. Maybe they're not as skilled at market analysis and problem-solving but terrific at relationship management and networking. Flip the script and tell them to interview you. Challenge them with a prompt like, "I want you to make sure you're a good fit as the VP of product for our company. You've got half an hour to ask me any questions you like." See where their mind goes, what their social skills are like, and how they think and would theoretically operate. The limited time shows you their general approach and even how they might work under pressure.

And never, never, never hire just to fill a spot. I've witnessed too many instances where companies end up with the wrong people on the bus and now need to get them off—but it's not always that easy. Desperation hiring is one of the most destructive practices I've ever seen. You're not just talking five to six figures of salary lost. That's hundreds of thousands of dollars in salaries, training costs, personnel hours, and headaches, frustrations, meetings, and turnover. On that last note, your valuable workers can't stand a poison pill shoved into their work environment. You're talking hundreds of thousands of dollars lost because you rushed the hiring process, and potentially more if you or your leadership don't have the guts to remove the person once it's clear they're a bad fit.

Keep in mind that your bench might be wide or deep depending on your needs. Say you've got plenty of budget to hire the positions you need. So you choose to bring on a number of people who specialize in those critical areas you've identified so they can build them up and make them better.

Or maybe you need to keep your bench small yet broad in abilities and interests. You need applicants with a range of skills who can fulfill four different roles at once. You're going to hire them very differently than you do the specialists. This makes it even more crucial that you test them up front rather than rely on checklists of hard skills.

In fact, in the new world of work, you'll likely see yourself hiring fewer salaried and hourly workers (full-time employees) and contracting more part-time professionals for specific tasks, deliverables, and projects, often for a set period. The COVID-19 pandemic has accelerated this.

Remember when hiring that EQ can be even more crucial than IQ. You need one smart department leader who knows what they're doing and can delegate tasks to others, but you need everyone in that department to have solid EQ so they can actually work together without bickering, competing, and ultimately quitting.

And remember that the world of work has changed. COVID-19 requires much more flexibility. Millennials and Gen Z don't want to be tied down to one company for the rest of their lives. In fact, they may not trust you if you try to push that line on them. They're realistic that they're going to work with you for a handful of years before pivoting to a new pathway. Engage that topic and ask them what they're looking to learn from your company, how they want to grow, and what skills they hope to polish or learn.

Talk frankly with your applicants about the new business world and how fluidity is the key to success. Those who get it will probably be a better fit, even if they don't match the checklist of hard skills. Be flexible in your requirements and let them know you're willing to train up their hard skills in exchange for them sharing their knowledge and unique mashup with your organization.

Companies Doing Fluidity Right

TaxJar: The Fluid Way to Hire

TaxJar bills themselves as "the leading technology solution for busy eCommerce sellers to manage sales tax."

They are a fully remote company that has created a tight-knit culture that has continued to thrive as they scale in size. With almost two hundred employees, the company is built foremost around putting the person at the center of everything. They are really in the business of finding, growing, and developing great people to put them against complex problems. With that as their ethos, you end up with a team built on trust.

And at TaxJar, they are in pursuit of better and want to demonstrate their intentionality around that.

Their mutual assessment process is a true reflection of that. They want their candidates to come and experience what it would be like to work with them so they feel like their environment fits with their life. It's designed as much of a way to give candidates the mutual opportunity to decide on them. Because one of TaxJar's values is about letting people shape their own destiny. So it's not only about TaxJar choosing someone from a values and skill set fit but also candidates choosing if this fits their lives as well.

Fors Marsh Group (FMG): The Fluid Way to Train Employees

FMG is a different kind of market research company built on helping companies thrive. They maintain a team of approximately three hundred employees, and accountability is a huge part of their core culture. And their processes for onboarding and employee growth are uniquely beautiful.

FMG takes an iterative approach to growth and development for their employees. They encourage dynamism and agility. And they focus on giving workers the support they need to grow.

One major difference is that FMG has shifted away from typical annual evaluations to continual performance discussions. This means continuous assessment and alignment for all of their employees at all levels. Their approach allows them to test and learn in various positions to see what works and what doesn't. The goal is to understand fit from a performance and interest perspective.

New employees still go through the traditional interview process. But then FMG puts them in a particular role initially based on skills, business need, and personal interest. They see how the worker performs in that initial role. They mutually assess how it's working and have a discussion around both parties' current and future desires. Then they work to match business needs with the employees' interests and goals.

Updating Your Organization for the New World of Work

By applying these five steps and managing your hiring process according to this new mindset, you should be able to easily upgrade your company with a more fluid approach.

It may not happen overnight, and there may be challenging conversations ahead. You may even feel intimidated. But now you've got a road map to translate the work you did on yourself into work for your company.

And it won't be as hard as you imagine. By reading this book, you've already proven you want to make your company better. While reading, you've learned how to do it. You have the knowledge. Now you just need to apply what you've learned.

You can do this.

CHAPTER 9

The Future Future of Work (and How to Find Your Place in It)

After reading this book, it should come as no surprise to hear the world is still changing. Constant change is what brought you to read this book in the first place. And that change is not slowing down.

No, the world is changing at an accelerating rate. It is more important than ever to remember to stay fluid. To "be water." None of us know what tomorrow will bring. A position once thought unassailable could be automated through a miracle advance in technology that no one saw coming. We'll soon advance from the new world of work to the *new* new world of work. From the future to the future future.

I've made it my mission to help people and the companies they work for reach their full growth potential. That's why I wrote this book: to prepare people like you to thrive amid the coming changes, to build your mashup, and to achieve your dreams.

Water in a glass temporarily takes the shape of its container. But when the glass is upended, the water doesn't stubbornly cling inside it. The water also does not retain the shape of the glass once it's been poured out. Instead, water spreads in the air as it pours. It hits the new surface with a splash and assumes a new form. And no one who walks into the room and sees that water imagines what the water looked like before.

Think about water in nature. Have you ever seen a river run perfectly straight from beginning to end? Rivers meander back and forth around hills, dip into valleys, and leap over cliffs in spectacular displays that tourists travel from neighboring countries to see. They flow endlessly toward their goal: "Every river flows to the sea," they say, which is a fancy way of saying that water never stops moving.

You've built your compass. You know where your sea is. You have the skills now to navigate around hills, to dive through valleys, and, when necessary, to take a leap of faith from cliffs that terrify others. You have what you need to survive in the new new world of work that's on its way.

But you can't close this book, turn out the light, and think that's enough. How do you stay fluid? How do you keep from turning stagnant? I urge you to go all the way back to the beginning of this book and review Chapter 3, Spotting the Trends. You must constantly continue to spot trends all the time everywhere you go. Gather information like a sponge and plot out your meandering course toward your sea.

What to Expect in the New New World of Work

As alien as the new world of work seems to some people, what's coming next will be another dramatic leap into a new way of living and working. The "job for life with minimal effort for maximum compensation" era will be long gone. The world moves far too fast and changes too swiftly for that now. You must prepare for your next leap.

The single job is being replaced by *all* workers building more than one income. "Revenue streams" will be the key phrase of the future. And each revenue stream will be set up to scale up or down as needed, or be created quickly and abandoned easily. Today's board member may tomorrow be a celebrity DJ, and the day after they'll be leading a non-profit for underprivileged youth. On the side, they'll sell motivational video courses, themed cookbooks, and professional music playlists cultivated to enhance specific events.

Think board members as celebrity DJs is too far-fetched? Then check out the Goldman Sachs CEO, David Solomon, and the recent *Rolling Stone* article about his electronic dance mixes. Yes, even the CEO of Goldman Sachs, who makes around $15 million per year as an executive, is out there expanding his mashup with a variety of cool flavors. He goes by D-Sol, which makes me wonder if the other Goldman Sachs executives call him that at board meetings. But he's following his passion and expanding his skill set. He knows all about the new new world of work, and he's fulfilling all of his interests.

In the past, business owners and companies thought and acted locally. Everything was about the smaller community. The new world of work now demands those business owners to think globally but still *act* locally. This means keeping an eye on the wider world for trends and solutions while still focusing on their immediate community.

But the new new world of work will require all to think and act globally. Our community has expanded beyond the boundaries of our neighborhood, city, state, province, or even nation. The whole world is connected now, and CEOs need to bear this in mind or be left behind.

Teams will become modular by nature. Companies won't be limited to how many people they can convince to move to one home office. Instead, they'll build teams all over the world—pockets of focused talent to complete tasks without regard for physical proximity. This means companies can draw the absolute best talents without wondering about immigration laws or uprooting families.

These teams will also be boundaryless—in location, time, and skills—with everyone on the team possessing a unique mashup of skills that will create boundaryless potential. The CEO may take a quick training from an employee to help manage a task and then turn it over to a third person for polishing. Rigid adherence to roles and hierarchies will threaten companies, but the organization that learns to flow without boundaries and arbitrary limits will thrive.

And the power and creativity of a company will be rooted in these hybrid workers. The more of these fluid mashuppers you have in your company, the greater the potential for more game-changing ideas. Imagine a company effortlessly switching between industries and absorbing whole new market niches with ease because their employees can instantly handle everything they encounter. This is a CEO's dream come true. Pivots become nearly effortless as your team simply shifts to accommodate the new tasks without fuss.

That's the true power of the mashup. Where one individual can move a mountain using fluidity, a fluid organization can move whole mountain ranges. The future requires us to use every part of ourselves to create our ultimate mashup and enhance our whole selves.

Even the way people grow has changed. Before, you had to learn and develop in sequential steps. Now you can run new skills and even roles in parallel. Mashing up the way you learn and weaving complementary skills together means you can grow even faster than before. That will help you adapt on the fly as you advance. New business models at an individual level that have now come to fruition give workers a whole new way to make a career.

With fpir generations in the workforce, we are at a critical inflection point where the whole work dynamic is going to change. The oldest millennials are around forty. In ten years, they will be running many of the major companies. Their whole approach and mindset to work will be different than that of generations past.

With a little patience and focused effort, anyone can shape themselves into the ultimate hybrid of both hard and soft skills. If you're fantastic at coding but can't speak to other people without tripping over your words, hire a career coach from a quick search on LinkedIn, or take an online course on professional communication from Udemy or Coursera. If you can network for days on end without tiring, but have no hard skills to speak of, build some through a similar online course or training. Research what skills are most in demand (flip back to the chapter on trendspotting to review) and go master them. Don't rely only on what you're naturally good at, but diversify yourself into the whole you with a range of skills and abilities that make you invaluable to every employer you meet. If you have three different companies from three different industries all offering you work, you're on the right path.

Eight Final Takeaways for the Journey Ahead

Apart from the general mindsets we've talked about so far, what else is going to change in the new new world of work? We'll see more globalization and more automation. Those changes alone indicate some pretty specific consequences. What can you expect, and what else can you do? Here are eight essentials to keep in mind.

1. Develop future-proof skills you can sell.

Don't spend valuable time and resources mastering a skill that's in danger of automation. Instead, cultivate skills (especially ones that require a human touch) that will stay in demand for some time. Soft skills are crucial for this reason because it's difficult to automate them. Hard skills are still important—just be aware that hard skills alone may leave you on shaky ground if you never cultivate new ones.

Learn a variety of hard skills throughout your life, and you can stay ahead of automation. Pick just one hard skill and lean on it for twenty years, and you're asking for trouble. As you know, people stuck in one solitary box, who never grow or cultivate themselves into anything new, will rapidly become unnecessary. The new world of work is not going to reward people with three college degrees focused in the same industry. The world changes so rapidly that many university degrees are obsolete upon graduation. And in this new world, a team can research most of that knowledge on the internet in a couple of minutes.

Instead of focusing purely on knowledge, build your soft skills and stay adaptable. Keep yourself necessary by becoming indispensable, and bosses will fall all over themselves to keep you.

Bear in mind that your target audience isn't just your neighborhood, your nation, or even your continent. Clients on the other side of the world in emerging nations and growing industries may desperately need your help building their new business. Keep growing. Keep your eyes open. Speaking of the other side of the world . . .

2. Build global relationships.

The world is a giant place, but it's getting smaller every day. The more global connections we build, the less the world is out of our reach. Keep your contacts open and broad. New industries and business locations open all the time. A small nation with little industry may one day explode into a technological giant in need of your exact mashup. How amazing would it be to help build a country?

When you're networking, don't think small. Think global. Spread your name and your business cards far and wide and stay open to extreme possibilities. You never know where you'll be in demand.

3. Embrace your whole self at work.

In the past, you only brought part of yourself (and even part of your full skills) to your workplace because of the narrow job you had to do. You fulfilled the other part through your hobbies and interests outside of work. Not anymore. It's important to now bring your whole self to work. That includes the right brain and left brain (i.e., soft and hard skills), your personal passions, and your professional interests. Your mashup is your whole self.

Every part of you is useful in fleshing out what your company can do. Those previously hidden parts of yourself could open up whole new avenues of revenue and networking. And you need to integrate every part of who you are, including the analytical and creative parts. We are no longer left-brain or right-brain workers. You need to bring your whole brain and whole self. Shift from being one dimensional into being multidimensional. Think of yourself as a Rubik's Cube—various sides make the whole. Be your full self at all times as you shift into a work-place mashup only you can create.

4. Make doing good a requirement.

My meaning here is twofold: do good work, and do good in the world.

You must produce results. Others are not going to hire you if you're known for slacking off, underperforming, or screwing up projects. But reputation goes beyond results. Your teams want someone who focuses on helping others, caring for people, and doing the right thing. It all goes back to a blend of both hard and soft skills. Employers are going to ask if you're good at what you do, but they'll also ask why you're good for the team and what you give to the people around you.

Don't just be the person who can make your company money. Be the person your coworkers look up to as a shining example. No technology can ever automate that.

This goes both ways. Employees also want to work for a company that does good. No one wants to work for the company that exploits the poor and marginalized. Knowing they're contributing to genuine good in the world is an added benefit many workers would take a pay cut to experience.

5. Make diversity in all things a priority.

Remember to diversify yourself like a stock portfolio. If one industry should close its doors for a while, you may not be able to advance there.

Be ready to shift somewhere else. Spread your network and your skills across many industries, so your biggest problem is choosing between opportunities instead of fighting others over one job opening.

Stay open to mindsets different from your own. Be ready to take on new perspectives, to work with people from a variety of backgrounds and approaches, and to not enforce your static way of business on others. Learn, adapt, and diversify your whole self at every opportunity.

6. Dissolve limits.

Limits are things we put on ourselves. We allow ourselves to be boxed in and told what we can and cannot do.

Of course, that's not you. Not anymore. The only thing stopping people from adapting and flowing like water is the belief that they can't. But the old boundaries are gone. You can reinvent yourself now, as long as you're willing to put in the time and effort.

When you find yourself needing to hire someone for a job, and that same limitation keeps popping up, consider learning to do that task yourself. It's obviously a skill that's in demand. Then you won't have to keep outsourcing your work or getting stuck waiting on someone else.

As you identify ways to keep growing in new directions, you change to fit the shape of the world's container. Never stop growing. And when you find a limit, consider it a challenge.

7. Look for new marketplace demands.

Entire industries will change as they are rebuilt and reimagined by younger and younger leaders. One day what it means to "go to the bank" will be completely different from what it is now, along with "get a job" and "write a résumé."

As younger generations shape our new new world of work, enormous opportunities are created for those willing to stand on the forefront of change. There are so many opportunities around you right now, and new opportunities come along every single day. This isn't a terrifying world but an exciting one. Look for opportunities to define the world and make yourself invaluable as a trendsetter.

8. Stay lean.

Companies don't want to be burdened with unnecessary workers or saddle themselves with enormous liabilities like pensions or guaranteed long-term contracts. Companies want to run lean so they can change and adapt. Every company wants to stay sleek and fast, even if their network becomes large.

The same is true of you. Don't weigh yourself down with heavy burdens that will prevent you from pivoting when needed. Ten-year contracts might not be in your best interest because who knows what even two years will bring? And don't take it personally if employers don't offer you a forever home. They're staying lean, and so should you.

How Your Story Might Pan Out

Some of these tips may seem like incredible tasks. To boost your focus and motivation, I've compiled a few examples below of people who have set themselves up with sustainable long-term career mashups. I've been honored to interview each of them on *Strategic Momentum,* and you can listen to their full interviews on my website if you want to hear more about their stories. They're incredible people and perfect examples of how to thrive in the new new world of work.

Like Chris Krimitsos, Starting Ugly

To illustrate the present state of Chris's career mashup, here are the titles Chris uses to describe the work he does:

Chief Creative Officer | Speaker | Author | Executive Producer | Business Leader

Chris grew up in New York with immigrant parents, and from an early age knew he wanted to be a business owner someday. He observed and learned from his uncles in the restaurant industry and was selling candy to his schoolmates by age twelve. He saw the positive impact entrepreneurs had on his community and decided he wanted to help the people around him in the same way.

Entrepreneurship was in his blood, and, as such, Chris was always starting and stopping things because he realized that that was an important part of learning what you like, what you don't like, and what you are good at. After multiple starts early in his career, he moved to Tampa, Florida, and got involved in real estate, successfully buying and flipping homes. While he was doing very well financially, he wasn't happy. His compass was pointing somewhere else.

So Chris set out to identify his purpose in life. He realized that he loved three things: helping people, community, and entrepreneurship. A mashup. This led him to creating a community for local business owners in the Tampa Bay area.

As a mastermind coordinator and strategist and a peer-to-peer mentoring facilitator, in addition to the many roles he also had, he focused on providing valuable resources through content, contacts, events, and education to help the Tampa Bay business owner community grow and thrive.

The success and experience of being that founder and organizer, and moving people forward toward economic growth, became the catalyst for his next pivot, which capitalized on another passion: technology.

Chris always had a knack for understanding trends (particularly in technology) and seeing their implications. So when podcasting emerged, he saw the greater potential to support and amplify people's voices and message through this powerful medium. So he founded another community- based media and event company, Podfest MultiMedia Expo. It's the world's number one interactive event for entrepreneurs, podcasters, and professionals that provides world-class education, ideas, and inspiration and a deeply supportive and strategic collective of people. But his career mashup also includes being an accomplished filmmaker, producer, and author.

As one who's had several entrepreneurial ventures that have been fundamental to his own self-discovery process, he's learned that "as you discover what you like, what you're strong at, what other people think you're good at, and what you want out of life . . . you could carve a niche in your ecosystem that's very fulfilling."

And that perspective is captured in his book *Start Ugly: A Timeless Tale About Innovation & Change*.

Chris's career advice is to find something you really enjoy doing and get a lot of reward out of because you'll enjoy doing it over and over. Because success to him is defined as being able to contribute and do something good in the world.

He's a truly fluid worker with a broad mashup story. And his passion for helping others ensures he stays out in front of rapid change so he can continue to motivate and inspire the people he cares so deeply about.

Like Eva Sadej, Managing Risk and Capitalizing on Opportunities

To show the variety of Eva's career mashup, here are her titles:

CEO | Founder | Forbes Business Council Member

Eva admits she's been testing and learning her whole life; spotting, managing, and padding risk; and always being one step ahead by working in parallel on multiple things to help her do so.

And like others in this book who have mastered a career mashup, Eva Sadej's story is an immigrant story. Born in Poland to a very traditional Polish family, Eva's family emigrated when she was a baby to the United States in 1993. She was raised " to cook and clean, and to be a housewife."

She also grew up with a more traditional view of career progression, and her career also started out that way initially. Given that her family didn't come from wealth, she worked hard and excelled in school so she could ensure she could get scholarships or financial aid. Her academic prowess led her to attending the acclaimed Stuyvesant High School in New York and then Harvard University studying Pre-Med as well as social psychology.

But then, charting the careers—and college debt—of her siblings in the medical field, Eva identified that she wanted to take a different path. She chose a career in finance to ensure financial independence out of college. She went on to join Bridgewater, one of the top hedge funds in the world and known for their culture of "radical transparency." She fortunately found an environment that tapped into her natural skills, interests, and elements of who she was as a person. It was a place that was trying to be the best at both management and investment yet with interesting social dynamics as part of their work culture.

What also appealed to Eva was the focus on systemization at Bridgewater. This process of creating repeatable success was second nature to her, as she drew from her experience as a champion runner in high school. The parallels between preparation, performance, and results in these fields meant she had also been able to leverage the mental toughness she had developed as an athlete into the business world.

Not only did Eva build her hard skills, she also added valuable social skills, like learning to be direct and intentional in communication. This augmented her foundational knowledge around people dynamics from her education in social psychology. All of which helped flesh out her understanding of how financial systems work and how humans can thrive.

During her four years at Bridgewater, Eva had a lot of different roles—it was a mashup of varied experiences, as she didn't know what she really wanted to do.

"I just didn't know what I was going to be doing. I was just trying to try things because when you're a young person, you just want to learn. And I was there to really learn.

"So everything bumped into another thing. It started in tech, but I wasn't that good at coding but I was reasonable at product management. There was a cool project and I got to lead that project. I understood process improvement, but I felt it was career limiting. So I went into investment and took the amazing world-class investment program. After I did that, I was just getting itchy being there for four years. So it was just a mishmash. It wasn't anything planful."

Through all these experiences, she learned that shape-shifting was critically important because with each new role she found it to be like a start-up. And this mashup of experiences was incredibly valuable on the next leg of her career journey, where she took the entrepreneurial leap inspired by her fiancé's successful whiskey subscription start-up, which started as a side hustle to his full-time job.

In her systemized way, she identified various start-up ideas that were twists on existing business models and did research on them (what she calls structured creativity). Her inspiration was Dry Bar, which identified the blowout as the most popular service in the hairdressing industry and then mastered it, disrupting the salon business and finding success in the process. Eva took this concept and looked for other fields to apply it, which led her to dental services.

She identified the clear need and an approach to solve it. But she also knew it wasn't about the idea but rather the execution. Shifting one's life to be an entrepreneur inherently had a lot of risk, so she hedged her risk by doing a career mashup—going to business school (mind you, it was Wharton) while also developing her business idea for Floss Bar. She parallel pathed business school while doing a bunch of pilots, learning and networking with others for her start-up until her business had a clear proof of concept. At that point, she chose to focus on Floss Bar full-time, which brings dental care to people too busy to make an appointment or who lacked transportation. That successful disruption of the dental industry also led her to being named a Forbes 30 under 30 recipient.

Yet COVID-19 brought immediate change and uncertainty. Eva had to be fluid in finding an alternative solution when Floss Bar's revenue plummeted to zero. Mobile dentistry wasn't a service that anyone was going to be gravitating toward in a pandemic. They were able to stand up a new business line—Med Bar—by being one of the first movers in delivering COVID-19 testing for essential workers. By rapidly pivoting, the traction for her business—now a health-care logistics company, has enabled her to expand her suite of services and create incredible business momentum and financial success.

Eva overcame family conditioning and cultural upbringing that pressured her to be rigid. She's a perfect model for how someone doesn't have to be set up from day one to thrive, but how they can learn fluidity at any age if they want it badly enough. She grew from a traditional starting place into a flexible yet humble and self-aware leader with a range of hard and soft skills that place her at the top of her game and the forefront of the new new world of work.

Like every start-up business that is a brand unto itself, Eva recognized that she too is a brand and as such has to see herself as a business. Her advice for those who are looking to craft the path that they want is that she encourages others—particularly if they are early in their career—to try something new and see what happens. Taking the risk in this case is worth it because when you look back you will be proud of yourself for just doing it.

Like Catharine Bowman, with Passion and Purpose

Here are Catharine's career mashup titles:

> Lymphedema Researcher | Medical Student | Speaker | Advocate | Association VP | Board Member

Catharine's career journey started early and was fundamentally driven by love. When she was eight years old, her mother was diagnosed with an aggressive form of skin cancer and underwent surgery to treat it. Despite the surgery, her mother developed a lifelong incurable lymphatic system disease, called lymphedema, that can cause severe swelling and discomfort that makes it difficult to move one's limbs. She witnessed her mother struggle not only physically but also psychologically, as there weren't any medical treatments available. Further, support communities for those suffering from the disease were nonexistent.

So she made a promise at eight years old to develop one of the first pharmacological treatments for the incurable disease. Catharine and her brothers were raised in a household that never set labels, and they were always encouraged to explore any interests they wanted to pursue. So she began studying every facet of the disease, not only from a medical perspective but the psychosocial elements as well.

Her discovery of a potential treatment was serendipity. She was reading a gardening magazine about the lupin flower, which had certain anti-inflammatory properties. Diving deeper into the active compounds of this flower, she connected the dots on how some of their properties could address the inflammation that occurs with lymphedema.

This eureka moment set her down the path to eventually becoming the world's youngest lymphatic researcher by the ripe old age of fifteen, all while attending high school. She was dynamically pivoting between deep specialization and broad education, and she successfully parallel pathed her educational and scientific career; Catharine says "they've beautifully aligned and melded together."

As someone who always thought big early on, she also inherently knew that making true progress was about breaking this big idea—and at times seemingly insurmountable pursuit—down into its smallest parts to create traction. By learning from these bite-size chunks and continuing to chip away at the iceberg, all of these small moments came together to help her create progress toward that bigger picture. Further, she knew the importance of networking, collaboration, and creativity—those soft skills that she continually developed and knew were essential to helping her get the momentum she needed.

Catharine was also naturally entrepreneurial. She always wanted to do more and think creatively about solutions. Thus she expanded her research beyond the bench science and pharmacology-based work.

She inherently understood the psychosocial challenges patients were dealing and inherently cared about the total human experience. So she expanded her work into the clinical side—understanding how people are affected by their lymphedema in terms of social, psychological, and financial elements—what she calls the life component. But it didn't stop there. She also moved into the surgical treatment of lymphedema and the health-care delivery side. She essentially created her own lymph-edema research mashup.

For Catharine, measuring the success of her compass wasn't rooted in hard, tangible metrics. It was a feeling where she could sense that alignment of her passion and purpose based on the goal she set for herself.

> When something really clicked for me, it was like this full body energy that had taken over that really made me feel like, "Okay. I am on the right path and I'm going to continue pursuing this path. And as much as I face barriers along the way, if I can remember why I'm doing what I'm doing in terms of compassion and connection and making a difference for people, I can overcome those barriers and continue on my journey."

It's her recognition of the human experience—that full customer journey of the person—and connecting all the dots along the way that was the fuel that helped her shape her own unique career mashup driven by passion, purpose, empathy, and ultimately love.

During her eight years as a lymphatic researcher, Catharine's career mashup has included the role of board member and VP of the Alberta Lymphedema Association, keynote speaker, medical student, and project lead. She's also been awarded the Forbes 30 under 30 in health care (she's only in her early twenties).

Her advice to those who are trying to create their ideal mashup that aligns to their own passion and potential involves three things:

- getting comfortable being uncomfortable and recognizing that is the pathway to change
- remember your intention and motivation as well as those core values that underlie your pursuits
- having courage in creating change

Like Mark Metry, Because There's No Other Choice

Mark has incredible diversity in his career mashup. Here are his titles:

Podcast Host | Founder | Author | Speaker | Course Creator | Board Member

Breaking out of your comfort zone can be challenging. For some, it's downright terrifying.

Mark Metry shares openly about battling trauma and social anxiety. His parents faced many challenges when they emigrated from Egypt to America and faced the stigma of being "outsiders." Though they only had $200 to their name, it was cultural difficulties that proved most pressing. They had to improve their English and adapt to a new culture quickly.

September 11 raised this tension to incredible levels unthinkable for a child. Mark grew up adapting and constantly redefining himself even as he faced bullying and abuse from those around him.

In fact, he developed various autoimmune-based health issues during childhood and adolescence like asthma, ADD, IBS, appendicitis, and insomnia. At the time he didn't realize this was the onset of his social anxiety.

Despite his trauma and pain, or perhaps because of it, Mark poured himself into the online world and especially into entrepreneurship. Back in 2011 he recorded YouTube videos of himself narrating video games in real time. Now this is commonplace, but back then, he was one of the first to do so. He quickly built a following and was able to garner ad revenue from it. He then became obsessed with *Minecraft* and, sensing opportunity for improvement, he then established the number one *Minecraft* server in the world and subsequently pulled down six figures—all as a young teen.

Mark had found alignment in what he loved while gaining an immense appreciation for the power of technology and community. But this early financial success didn't address or solve his internal struggles. College was harder as he fell into depression and grappled with the ongoing anxiety, stress and deep pain he was experiencing stemming from his childhood.

> I was living in so much fear that by the time I was eighteen, I began to just try to kind of like escape the pain that I was in with alcohol, drugs, partying, definitely

food was my vice of choice. And I remember this time where I had gained a ton of weight in a short period of time. And next thing I know, I'm obese. I'm 220 pounds. My lifelong social anxiety transforms into social isolation. And I really get depressed seriously for the first time in my life. That eventually led me to being suicidal for about a month of my life towards the end of 2015. And that was the foundation in which I used to just totally go on the offense of my life and change everything around.

After falling into the deepest part of his depression, Mark realized there was nowhere to go but up. To overcome his social anxiety, he began his quest to become "Human V2.0" by taking small steps and repeating them until he felt comfortable taking on more. And this involved both mental *and* physical health.

He forced himself to break out of that comfort zone bit by bit, which served as a catalyst to then start an acceleration agency, VU Dream, which was on the edge of the growing exponential technologies industry. At nineteen, he then created his successful *Humans 2.0* podcast, a Global Top 100 show for entrepreneurs about the modern technological context of the world. Its goal is to provide anyone with the tools they need to develop themselves on a regular basis.

This led to him parallel pathing these roles as a TedX keynote speaker, consultant, educator, and then eventually adding on the title of author to his talent stack. Now, he's championing "brain health" wherever he can through his book *Screw Being Shy: Learn How to Manage Social Anxiety and Be Yourself in Front of Anyone* as part of his continually growing career mashup.

Through it all, Mark has built a range of skill sets. He confronted his gaps and challenges and learned to overcome them. He built both his hard and soft skills until no one could equal his unique mashup. And then he turned outward to helping others.

But he hasn't stopped there. Mark wants "to change the world by giving people the tools, systems, experiences, and activities to start growth-minded podcasts at scale to impact more people" through his new podcast acceleration company Growcasts, which is a mashup unto itself.

With as fast and furious as he's going, his career advice is to pause every once in a while to reevaluate things and gain perspective, which will help you go much further. "If you want to go far, you've got to go deep."

Mark serves as an excellent example of the modern fluid human being. His story shows that you can overcome those deep barriers and fears and create the momentum you are looking for.

Now It's Your Turn

The future of work is coming. But you know what to expect, and you're ready to face it.

Here's what you need to remember:

Study your trends. Don't shut your eyes or stop paying attention. The world is changing around you, and you need to see where you're going.

Heed your compass. You created your guide. You know how to flow like a river to your sea. When you're lost, consult your compass. Pay attention to it at every decision point and do what is truly best for your future.

Prepare for change. You may think you've got all your fears and worries out. Then, surprise! You react with terror to a new opportunity. Maybe you're suddenly faced with a leap of faith off a cliff into a whole new industry. Breathe. Prepare yourself for the change. Remember all the challenges you've already overcome. Then look to the future and follow your path toward your sea.

Network. Engage with others as you work toward your goal. Don't stop making connections. Today's lunch buddy could be tomorrow's lifeline. Yesterday's protégée could be tomorrow's boss. You never know what's coming, and the more allies you have, the better connected you'll be when it comes time to pivot and grow.

Up level your skills. Don't stop learning and growing. You are a thriving organism that must keep moving in order to stay alive. Keep flowing like water, keep adapting to new containers, and never forget that the next container is just around the corner. Sharpen your skills in your spare time, diversifying the portfolio that is your skill set.

Together, these five elements of the mashup system will create a flywheel of progress you can ride for the rest of your career—and life.

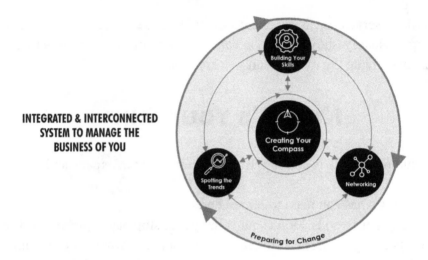

If you're looking for more resources to guide you along the road, this isn't the end. My *Strategic Momentum* podcast lets you hear me interview dozens of progressive leaders and entrepreneurs and reveal all their secrets to success. This book is only the beginning. There's a whole new world waiting for you out there. And now you know how to access it.

You have everything you need to not only survive but thrive in the new new world of work. I may see you out there somewhere. Feel free to say hello. I'd love to network with you. Who knows? We may even end up working together.

Do you feel that? The tension, the excitement? A million opportunities are waiting for you. And you have the road map to success.

You're ready. Now go be water.

Let's build the business of you together.

Change is here. Uncertainty is the new certainty. But what happens now . . . and next? Let's continue your journey to get you to where you want to go.

The *Building the Business of You* companion course features instruction from me along with business, communication, and networking experts who offer actionable advice and diverse perspectives from real-world experiences.

In this guided course, we'll dive deeper into the system so you can put these concepts into practice. We'll work through the "how" so you can find your flow and form your unique career mashup. Specifically, you will . . .

- spot the trends so you can identify not just "what" but the "so what" and "now what"
- create your compass (or compasses) to point you where you want to go
- prepare for change so you can push past fear and inertia
- network in a way that builds authentic relationships to support you in your journey
- build the skills to move you towards your goals

Go to www.BizOfYou.co to pick up where this book leaves off and continue aligning your passion, purpose, and potential.

Acknowledgments

To create momentum, it takes a village of support.

When you have a kernel of an idea, it's those discussions with others that help you craft, shape, and hone that eventual thesis which eventually solidifies what you know in your gut to be true. Yet it's also their excitement and fundamental belief in what you are doing based on their own career journeys that propel you forward.

To my wonderful husband, Josh, who has been instrumental in my personal and professional growth. You've pushed me to reach higher, further, and faster with my goals than I would have ever imagined— thank you for your ongoing encouragement and patience.

Thanks to my amazing team, Alexis Anthony and Alan Corcoran, who have been my sounding boards every step of the way. Your ongoing enthusiasm and perspectives have accelerated my vision of what's possible.

Dan Yu and Marc Angelos—masterminding with you (and that's before I even knew that's what we were even doing) has been a bright spot during an otherwise challenging period in 2020. Your ongoing insights, advice, and support have meant the world to me. It's that true value exchange that lifts everyone up.

To my mother-in-law, Diana Seiler—your unconditional love and desire to help me realize my vision is beyond words. Your selflessness, compassion, and empathy toward others, no matter who they are, is what we need more of in this world.

Finally, thank you to all my podcast guests, who have given me so much inspiration and insight into the world of work and have been an underlying driver for bringing these concepts to life.

Strategic Momentum Featured Guests

The following individuals were interviewed on *Strategic Momentum* and made an appearance in this book. Visit their site or profile to learn more about their career mashup journey.

Name	Website
Marc Angelos	www.anvictus.com
Mehtab Bhogal	www.kartaventures.com
Jenny Blake	www.pivotmethod.com/about-jenny
Catharine Bowman	www.linkedin.com/in/catharinebowman/
Dana Cavalea	www.danacavalea.com
Bhavna Dave	www.linkedin.com/in/bhavnadave/
Scott DiGiammarino	www.moviecomm.com
Stephane Fitch	www.fitchink.com
Beth Freedman	www.linkedin.com/in/bethfreedman/
Meghan French Dunbar	www.meghanfrenchdunbar.com
Kevin Garton	https://www.linkedin.com/in/kevingarton/
Annette Grotheer	www.theshopdocs.org
Jordan Harbinger	www.jordanharbinger.com
Yao Huang	www.hatchery.vc
Erin King	www.erinking.com
David Knies	www.dknies.com
Chris Krimitsos	www.chriskrimitsos.com
Jon Krinn	www.clarityvienna.com
Rick Lindquist	www.leguphealth.com

Name	Website
Dr. Mary Lamia	www.marylamia.com
Crate Media	www.crate.media
Mark Metry	www.markmetry.com
Joanie Rufo	www.initiateconsulting.com
Eva Sadej	www.medbar.com, www.flossbar.com
Joe Saul-Sehy	www.stackingbenjamins.com
Kim Scott	www.radicalcandor.com
Deepak Shukla	www.deepakshukla.com
Lee Sommers	www.ppf-fitness.com
Jennifer Trzepacz	www.linkedin.com/in/jetrzepacz/
Kareen Walsh	www.kareenwalsh.com
Michael Wilkinson	www.leadstrat.com
Dan Yu	www.fastbookadvisors.com
Cara Silletto	www.magnetculture.com

About the Author

Connie Steele is a seasoned marketing and strategy executive, co-founder of Flywheel Associates, and host of the Strategic Momentum Podcast. Connie has always been intrigued by the "why" behind companies and careers that thrive. With over twenty years of combined Fortune 500, mid-size company, and startup experience, she has observed firsthand how business is no longer binary, hierarchical, or absolute but non-linear, collaborative, and fluid.

Connie is also the author of *Building the Business of You: A System to Align Passion and Growth Potential Through Your Own Career Mashup*, the first book to help professionals and entrepreneurs navigate the new world of work while aligning personal passions, interests and professional advancement. Her career mashup advice has appeared on Thrive Global. Hear Connie interview founders, creatives and executives who share valuable tips, stories and advice around understanding the business of work at www.StrategicMomentum.co.